FOREWORD

This book is a compilation of (nearly) every single tried murder or manslaughter, attempted or successful, that occurred within the City of Manchester between 1890 and 1899. There are two inspirations for this book I must acknowledge; Michala Hulme's *A Grim Almanac of Manchester*, and Boar and Blundell's *The World's Greatest Unsolved Crimes*, which influenced the story-telling theme of the book as well as its subject matter.

To write *Murders in Manchester*, I have used criminal records, censuses, newspapers and burial records, with credit especially to the *Manchester Evening News* and *Manchester Courier*. I am thankful not only to these resources, but to my family and friends who have had to hear me talk about this book endlessly, and to myself, for my own dedication and commitment to what was, essentially, a thankless and pointless task.

Thank you for purchasing this book, and please await further issues, by decade, of the *Murders in Manchester* series.

In memory of: Neil James, James Cottrell and Doris Hilditch, Roland and Elsie Holmes, Walter Charles and Catherine Sangster, Joseph and Rose-May Saxton.

TABLE OF CONTENTS

CHAPTER
1. THE BABY IN THE MERSEY..3
2. THE AXEMAN OF REDDISH..6
3. THE BABY IN THE BED..8
4. THE SON-IN-LAW STABBING..9
5. THE MAD MAN AND HIS WIFE..12
6. THE BESWICK BEGGAR..15
7. THE BABY IN HULME..18
8. THE WORKHOUSE CHOPPER..18
9. THE ANCOATS INHERITANCE..19
10. THE LANDLADY'S SON...23
11. THE RICE PUDDING KILLER..26
12. THE BABY OF TIB STREET...33
13. THE LONGSIGHT SHOTGUN...34
14. THE HANGING DAUGHTER..36
15. THE HULME AMMONIAC..37
16. THE WELSH HARP QUARREL...39
17. THE BROTHERS OF ANCOATS...40
18. THE DEVINE INCIDENT...44
19. THE BABY OF DEANSGATE..46
20. THE HULME FAMILY BUSINESS..47
21. THE ROCHDALE ROAD GANG..51
22. THE COLLYHURST FIRE..53
23. A BETTING MAN FLEES THE SCENE...................................57
24. THE PUNCH AT DEANSGATE..59
25. THE BABY IN THE PEGGY TUB...62
26. THE CANAL STREET SCUTTLE...65
27. THE AXE AT ANCOATS..71
28. THE WORKHOUSE BABY DROWNED..................................73
29. THE RUSHOLME SPUD...75
30. THE IRRITATED NEIGHBOUR..77
31. THE PARCEL IN THE CANAL..80
32. THE STAIR CASE...84
33. TEMPER LOST IN GORTON..86
34. THE BROTHERS OF PICCADILLY...90
35. THE DRUNKARD AND THE LAMP.......................................92
36. THE HAMMER AT REDDISH..94

37. THE BABE IN THE WOODS..97
38. NEGLECT ON POTT STREET...99
39. NEGLECT ON PETER STREET...101
40. THE CLEGG STREET BABY...106
41. THE BRADFORD BUS...108
42. 'SOMETHING TO DO'..110
43. THE SMASHED WINDOW...114
44. THE ANCOATS BOATMEN..116
45. THE WATCHMAKER'S DELUSION......................................118
46. THE BIRCH BROOK BABY..121
47. THE MURDER AT THE STATION.......................................122
48. THE UNFAITHFUL WIFE...127
49. THE WIFE USHER..132
50. THE DANCER'S FINALE...133
51. THE FALSE SPIRIT OF CHORLTON...................................136
52. GOSSIP ABOUT THE BOSS..139
53. THE CHORLTON STREET WAREHOUSE.........................141
54. THE BRICKLAYER'S BABY...149
55. THE CLOUT AT HARPURHEY..152
56. THE THROAT CUTTER...158
57. THE LIVERPUDLIAN...159
58. THE CHRISTMAS QUARREL..161
59. THE NEW YEAR'S BRAWL...163
60. THE DEATH OF THOR..164
61. THE OLD TRAFFORD SHOOTING.....................................166
62. A FIGHT OUT OF HAND...168
63. THE PENKNIFE IN BESWICK..170
64. THE POOR GIRL OF CRUMPSALL....................................172
65. THE BROTHER AND THE BROOMSTICK.........................174
66. THE UNHAPPY LODGERS...176

1.
THE BABY IN THE MERSEY
22 Nov 1889

Shropshire native Elizabeth Mapp (24) had been in the Stockport Union Workhouse since May 1889, her baby son Edward having been born in April. She left the Workhouse on November 19th, both her and her son being strong and healthy. She slept in a closet that night. On November 20th, Mapp turned up at the home of Ann Kershaw on Arlington Square, Stockport, asking for a bed for her and Edward. She stayed there for 3 days, during which Edward cried a lot, and Mapp often gave him something out of a bottle.

On November 22nd, she left the house, ostensibly to take Edward to a doctor. She walked for hours through some fields with her baby wrapped in a shawl, then threw him into the river Mersey near Barlow Moor Hall, Chorlton-cum-Hardy to *'put him out of his misery'*. He died within a minute after moving his hands about in the water. She stayed there for about 15 minutes before leaving the scene.

She saw the lamp from a watchman's cabin behind her; the watchman let her stay there on the condition that she would give details to the police when they arrived. The following morning at 12:30am, Sgt. Lynn found her in the watchman's cabin on Wilbraham Road, Chorlton. He talked to her and returned at 3:30am, finding her asleep on the cabin's seat. Her hand was bleeding, and her clothes were wet and dirty. He woke her and asked what the bundle behind her contained.

She correctly told him it was full of skirts. She refused to give her name and address, and was taken to the local police station. She had in her possession a gold watch, albert chain, a baby's skirts and 6s. 10½d. in cash. She was brought before the magistrates the same day but still refused to give a name.

Superintendent Bent ordered the river to be dragged and local pits to be searched, suspecting the baby to be drowned. Later that day Bent cautioned her, and she gave a statement. She said she was becoming exhausted with the baby's crying, but did not want to give it away. She took Bent to where she drowned the child. The next day she was charged with murder.

On the 5th of December she appeared in Manchester County Police Court, and pleaded guilty. With Superintendent Bent asserting there was no evidence that this was true, she was remanded for a week. The body was found on the morning of December 19th by James Johnson, of Ciss Lane, Urmston, who was walking along Broken Bank and saw Edward fastened by his clothes to a pile in the bed of the river. On December 20th, she was shown the body on her request. She said *"Oh, my darling,"* and picked him up and kissed him, then said *"This is my child, I have done it, I suppose I must suffer for it"*.

Bent heard her say she would suffer anything for her baby. On December 23rd, an inquest was held by district coroner Frederick Price at the Talbot Hotel, Stretford. Dr. Alfred Bailey Liptrot examined the baby in the hotel's stables.

It was badly decomposed, clothed, and had died from shock of immersion. It was in a very weak state. One juror asked if Mapp had been tested for insanity; the coroner said this was not the issue of the inquest. The jury unanimously returned a verdict of murder. She was sentenced to death on March 6th 1890 at Manchester Assizes. This was reduced, over the course of 5 years, through petitions and correspondence with the Home Office and the Queen. On March 10th, the Stockport Board of Guardian's weekly meeting brought up a discussion about Mapp's case. W Barber, of Stockport, attested for her good character while in the workhouse, while J Rowcroft, of Hyde, brought up the fact she was a Sunday school teacher, and was probably temporarily demented by her time in the workhouse. He moved that the clerk draw up a petition to be signed by the Board; the assistant clerk rejected this, saying the Board could sign it individually but not as an entire organisation. On March 12th, a telegram from Sydney Gedge, a Stockport member, attracted public support for her, and the Stockport Guardians sent a petition for reprieve to the Home Secretary. On the morning of March 13th, Strangeways governor Maj. Preston received word from the Home Secretary commuting the death sentence. On March 19th, a meeting of the committee behind the movement to commute her sentence was held in Manchester; the meeting decided that petition sheets would be put in churches.

On March 21st the Home Secretary wrote to solicitors Millar and Leak, informing them that their petition to reprieve Mapp had worked; the Secretary of State agreed the sentence would be commuted to penal servitude for life. By March 27th 15,721 signatures had been gathered in her support, including barristers and councillors.

2.
THE AXEMAN OF REDDISH
26 Dec 1889

Joseph Brindley, a steamer at Bradshaw, Hammond & Co. printworks, struck his wife Mary on the crown of her head from behind with an axe as she got up at around 5:00 on a Thursday morning at their home of 166 Gorton Road, Reddish. She had thought he was reaching down to get his stockings, but was suddenly repeatedly attacked. The blow cut through two pins that bound a large twist of her hair, and, with other chops, made 8 or 9 incised wounds on the skull. He took a table knife, put her in a headlock under his left arm and made a wound 4 inches long but only an eighth inch deep on her throat.

He attacked her again, cutting her lip and scratching her throat. A struggle ensued, with her grabbing the knife from his hand and throwing it on the landing. He tried to drag her towards the knife, but failed; he tried to throw her over the bannister, and failed again. Inch by inch they fought until they got to the top of the stairs, where he tried to push her towards the bedroom. She grabbed onto the bannister rails, but eased her grip so they both fell down the stairs.

He tried to drag her into the kitchen, but was getting exhausted. She made her way to the front door and onto the steps, where her cries of *"murder!"* brought the assistance of labourer Thomas Hargreaves. She was bleeding and completely exhausted and apparently fainted; she was *"falling over when she got to him"*, still in her bloody nightdress. At one point, she shouted *"Oh, Joe, do not kill me!"* This prompted her neighbour John Thornley, a brewer, to get dressed and rush out, where he helped Hargreaves to sit her on a chair in her house. Thornley shouted Joseph down, who was in the scullery upstairs, washing himself. He came down and was

casually smoking a pipe by the time Police Sgt. Smith arrived a few minutes later.
She asked him why he did it: he said *"through jealousy"*. Smith found a blood-stained axe with its head detached from its handle in the bedroom. He was taken into custody. On the way to the court the same morning he asked *"Will this be a 6 months' job? I do not know what made me do it."* Thornley sent for Dr. Hanson Smith, familiar with the victim, who said that Mrs. Brindley was in a semi-conscious state when he arrived, with a practically non-existent pulse and severe shock. She had four wounds and several bruises on her throat. Some of the cuts on her head had badly hit the bone of her skull. He confirmed she was out of danger. He was understood to be *"quiet, inoffensive"* and with *"sober and industrious habits"*. He was remanded at the Manchester County Police Court on the January 2nd 1890, with his wife being unable to appear.

On the 8th, she appeared at the same court, looking very ill and seated in the witness' box. She said that at about midnight on Christmas Day, her husband asked if there was any tea in the pot. She said she thought there was, so he went downstairs and came back some minutes later. He was restless in bed and complained of feeling ill. That morning, she said he should go to work; he said he would take the week off due to feeling unwell. She complained that he did not work enough, and she would find work for herself to feed their children if he would not.
Then the attack began. Joseph claimed to have no recollection of the event; he said he was very sorry, but asked no questions and made no comments. Browning, Joseph's manager, attested for his good character, and promised to attend before the judge at the trial at the assizes to defend him further.
He was given 4 months hard labour on March 5th.

3.
THE BABY IN THE BED
17 Jan 1890

The newborn son of cook Eleanor Swann, wife of Arthur, was suffocated between the flock bed and mattress on which it was born at 36 Howard Street, Eccles New Road, Salford in the home of her employer, Major Sheringham of the 2nd Battalion, Cheshire Regiment. That noon, she told another servant, Eliza Parren, that she felt unwell, and went upstairs to bed. At 3:30pm Parren went to see how she was; Swann said *"Do you know I have had a baby?"* Parren said *"No, where is it?"*

Swann pointed to the bed, which Parren lifted to see the shocking spectacle of the child's 'quite dead' body wrapped in an old black dress. Dr. Wilson of Broad Street, Pendleton made a post-mortem examination and found the baby's body to be well-developed, but his face was bruised and livid and the back of his skull was pressed violently onto the brain. He could not say whether the death was accidental.

The district coroner Frederick Price held an inquest at the Clowes Hotel, Salford on the 22nd; addressing the jury he suggested an open verdict should be returned, and if the police were not satisfied they could take Swann before the magistrates. The jury decided there was not enough evidence to make a decision, but agreed the death was from suffocation.

4.
THE SON-IN-LAW STABBING
8 Mar 1890

Alexander Sorbie (67), from Paris, was a tailor for a firm on York Street. He lived with his Irish wife Elizabeth and their son and daughter at 12 Marsden Court, a narrow court off Fennel Street in central Manchester. This court was behind modern buildings and was obscured from public view. Another of his daughters, Emily was married to a slipper maker Charles William Hampson (26) of 17 Tebbutt Street, Rochdale Road. At about 8:40pm on a Saturday evening, Hampson and Emily went to see her parents. All of them were drunk except Emily and her sister.

The son Albert (14) was apparently not there. They began to quarrel about a half crown that Hampson accused Emily of taking from his pocket; they had apparently been fighting about this before they had arrived. Sorbie went to lie on the sofa he usually slept on. The quarrel grew louder; Sorbie said he would not have Hampson making a disturbance in the house. Hampson refused to leave, to which Sorbie *"put his fist in his face"* and said he would make him leave.

Hampson continued to refuse to leave, saying he would go when he was ready. Sorbie said *"Why do you come to my house to make your bother? Why do not you go home to do it?"* He threatened to call for a policeman, and went and put on his jacket and waistcoat. He put his hand in his waistcoat pocket. Hampson went after him and a struggle took place. They were separated, and Mrs. Sorbie interfered; Hampson pushed her down. Emily and her sister pulled Hampson off Sorbie.

Mrs. Sorbie went to the door to call for police, when Hampson grabbed her and held her behind the door. Emily tried to get between them; Sorbie ran up and made a single underhand stab

below Hampson's left groin with a small pocket knife. It pierced 2½" deep and made a wound 1½" long. Hampson said *"You coward!"* three times. Sorbie was holding the knife after this, and said nothing.
Neighbours heard loud voices, and the door being thrown open. Mrs. Sorbie left the house, followed by Hampson (with Emily's and her sister's help). The door was locked from the inside. Hampson staggered into the court and leaned against the wall ceiling facing the house, and told Emily *"Fetch a policeman, I am dying."* She tried to find a policeman, but could not; she returned to see him lying on the flags, bleeding profusely.

PC Green arrived and was given an account by Thomas Fennell (24 Marsden Court). He went to the house to see Hampson unconcious, his thigh bleeding badly. He took Sorbie to Albert Street police station. A young man had fetched a cab; four policemen came and put Hampson into it, and took him to the Royal Infirmary. He arrived there just before 9:00pm; he was attended to by resident surgeon Edmund Taylor Milner. The main vein of the thigh had been badly wounded; he was dangerously low on blood. A transfusion was attempted, but he never regained consciousness and died 2 hours later at 11:05pm, from the shock of blood loss. Emily went home and found the half-crown on the hearthrug. An inquest was held on March 10th by deputy City coroner Sidney Smelt. Sorbie attended, *"grey-haired and shabbily-dressed"*. Emily was called upon; she told her story, and said that when Sorbie put his hand in his pocket, he did not remove the knife. She said Hampson and her father often quarrelled but never physically fought. Smelt said strong evidence would be required to warrant his committal for wilful murder, but he did not see how the jury could help sending Sorbie to trial for manslaughter.

The jury returned the verdict of manslaughter. That afternoon he was brought before J Lomax at the City Police Court, and was committed to the Liverpool Assizes for manslaughter; he was there acquitted, and returned to 12 Marsden Court.

5.
THE MAD MAN AND HIS WIFE
21 Jun 1890

On Friday, June 20th, Edward Young (35), a jobbing joiner for a firm on Hamilton Street, Collyhurst and father of 8, came home to 8 Worrall Street, Collyhurst at about 7:00pm, quite sober and friendly having been paid that day, and complained to his wife Esther (34) that his leg was paining him. He went to bed 2 hours later, and his wife and daughter Maud (12) followed at about 11:00, when his wife brought him some beer on his request. He started smoking his pipe; his wife told him to stop, or she would leave. At about 1:00am the next day, he cut her throat and breast with a knife (table, tanner's or shoemaker's) in bed. She said *"Oh, Ted, what are you doing? Oh, Ted, do not!"* Maud, awoken, went to the room and saw her father turning off the lamp. She asked *"What did you do to my mother?"* He replied, *"Oh, nothing."*

She turned on the lamp and shook her mother, and saw her covered in blood. She ran with the baby to her mother's sister Elizabeth O'Neill's house in Harrowby Street, telling her *"Dada has stabbed mama again"*. On the way, they met a policeman, and took him to the house. He gave himself in at the charge office at Willert Street police station *"with bare head and feet"* at 1:10, telling Inspector Hyde he had killed his wife.

He had had a drink, but was not drunk. When police arrived, they found her body in bed, practically dead, with their baby next to her, covered in blood but uninjured. A large knife covered in blood was found in the bedroom. She died within 15 minutes. He was taken to Goulden Street police station, where he was charged by Superintendent Godby; he told him *"I will not say anything at present"*.

He was taken to the City Police Court on the coroner's warrant the same day, where the Stipendiary Magistrate remanded him until the 26th. He said *"I have often thought I would do for her, but I have never had the courage. However, I have done it now."* When formally charged, he said nothing. On June 23rd, the inquest was held by deputy City coroner Sydney Smelt at the City Coroner's Court. The first witness was their daughter Maud, 12, who said that her father was generally mean to her mother; she often slept at her sister's, and had in February finished his 3 month sentence of hard labour for stabbing her in bed.

About nine weeks before the murder, he asked for a lost razor, and when he found it there was a struggle between him and Esther, who threw the razor out of the window to protect herself. After this he was absent for three weeks. He often would threaten to choke her or cut her throat. He used to drink heavily but was recently sober. He had been off work for 6 days the week before the murder due to a sprained foot.

He was not always employed, and earned a 'precarious' living. He was described by an acquaintance as a man *"who could not take a glass of beer and stop there"*. He was described as *"morose at times, and given to fits of absent-mindedness"*, and was often absent from work when drinking. He was medium height, with a dark complexion and black moustache. His wife was *"a lively little woman, well-liked by her neighbours"*.

After more testimony from another daughter, 14, the jury returned the verdict of wilful murder. While in custody he complained of head pains and requested a doctor often. He complained people were watching and laughing at him, and would look under his bed for no apparent reason. He was indicted at the Manchester Summer Assizes on July 16th. A co-worker claimed he was never drunk, but was very absent-minded; he once searched for a plane that was right next to him, and often claimed someone was stealing his tools. His sister Mrs. Kersall and brother-in-law Lewis O'Neill gave testimony.

Kersall claimed he once threw a glass of beer into a fire and immediately forgot he did it, and sometimes refused to talk to her for hours at a time. O'Neill claimed he had only seen this strange behaviour when he was drunk. Another brother-in-law said he had once passed Young in the street, and Young ignored him for no reason.

Another co-worker, Henry McBride told the court that Young once complained that when he could not sleep, strange thoughts came into his head. Medical superintendent HR Lev of the Prestwich Asylum said his inspections of Young on July 3rd and 4th concluded that he was of sound mind. Rvd. Denis Shehan said he knew the family, and saw Young's strange behaviour. Mr. and Mrs. John Nolan, publicans of the Locomotive Inn on Marshall Street, attested to his sobriety, quietness and inoffensiveness.

Dr. F Lee of Rochdale Road said he had told the prisoner to see about being admitted to a lunatic asylum in November. Young claimed he had committed the murder in an act of frenzy. On August 1st he spoke to 3 of his children. One of them, a 9-year-old girl, was adopted by a Parisian convent, which he was pleased with because he had been listening to the priest every day while in prison. Apparently Collyhurst was generally supportive of Young, and was pleased to hear the sentence respited. He was due to be executed on August 5th while in Strangeways. A letter from the Home Secretary on August 2nd instructed that he be sent to Broadmoor.

6.
THE BESWICK BEGGAR
30 Jun 1890

At 12:00pm on a Monday afternoon, Ellen Rogers (4 Sawley Street, Beswick) had a man knock at her door. She let him in, and he asked to sit down. She prohibited it, because he looked '*wild*', and she was afraid of him. Between 2:00pm and 3:00pm he was seen roaming aimlessly around Albany Street, Beswick, apparently drunk. Butcher Frederick William Brown (8 Solent Street, Beswick) saw the man on the corner of nearby Devon Street. A quarter of an hour later he saw the man trying to open a door on Viaduct Street, and then go into a pub. At about 3:00pm he walked up nearby Hillkirk Street, followed by a large crowd. James Conduit (24 Albany Street, Beswick), a boiler maker at Galloway's on Hyde Road, went up to the man and took him by the back of his coat collar, and said *"what's your little game?"*.

He kicked him between the legs; the man fell down, and Brown picked him up. This happened 3 times. Brown led the kicked man away a short distance, who began exclaiming that someone was going to shoot him. Brown let him go. At 3:05pm PC Joseph Whitehead saw the kicked man being followed by a large crowd on nearby Devon Street. He followed him and the crowd to Albany Street, where he collapsed.

The man indicated to Whitehead where he had been kicked. He got the man to his feet and started walking with him, but he collapsed. Whitehead found another policeman, and they put the man in an ambulance to Brook Street station, Bradford, about half a mile away. He died almost instantly upon being put in the vehicle, and was placed in the station mortuary. Whitehead went to Conduit's house; he was in bed. He charged him with causing the man's death by kicking his abdomen, and Conduit replied *"I know nothing about it"*. He took him to Brook Street station, where Inspector Wild was on duty. Initially Conduit denied the accusation, and then gave Wild a statement, claiming he had seen the man loitering, and he and his neighbours suspected him of being a housebreaker.

He went to ask the man what he was after and received an unsatisfactory response; he then gave the man a shove and a kick to move him along, but did not intend to hurt him. Sgt. Brodrick made inquiries that led to Conduit's arrest that same day.

On the morning of July 1st he was charged at the City Police Court, before Mr. Parlane, with causing the man's death. Wild asked for, and was granted, a remand until July 3rd, with bail being refused.

The next day, the *Manchester Courier* described the unknown decedent as *"between 40 and 50… 5ft. 7in. high, with dark brown hair and moustache, heavy dark eyebrows, and beard of about two day's growth. There is a scar on the left side of his neck, and the face is pock-marked. The deceased was dressed in a dark brown check coat and vest, mixture check trousers, grey worsted stockings, lace-up boots, black pot hat, grey union army shirt."*

On July 2nd, an inquest was held by deputy City coroner Sidney Smelt at the City Coroner's Court. The man was identified as John Lindsay (35 Longworth Street, Deansgate), a 46-year-old betting man. Matthew Keenan, with whom Lindsay lodged, said Lindsay had been in bed from June 27th to June 29th following a drinking binge, which he apparently did frequently. WJ Heslop, divisional police surgeon, said that his post-mortem had found two slight bruises on the right knee, and another slight bruise, 3" long, on the left. All of his principal organs were diseased; the mucous membrane of the stomach was rotten from alcoholism.

He proposed the cause of death to be alcoholism, possibly hastened by the shock of the kicking. Other witnesses asserted Lindsay had attempted to enter Conduit's house before the kicking. Wild attested to Conduit's usual good behaviour. After hearing all the evidence, Heslop believed the cause of death was the kicking, and the man was sick from delirium tremens. After some deliberation the jury returned a verdict of manslaughter. Smelt asked if the magistrates had taken bail; Inspector Hyde said that they had refused bail until after the hearing on July 4th. Smelt said he would take any bail which the magistrates took. The hearing of July 4th took place before H Phillips and TT Shann, with Conduit being represented by R Cobbett.

He was committed for trial on a charge of manslaughter, with bail being allowed. He appeared at the Manchester Assizes before Mr. Justice Vaughan Williams on July 15th; he was described as a *"powerful, middle-aged man"*. He was defended by Mr. Shee, and Mr. Cottingham prosecuted. Ellen Rogers, Brown, Lindsay's mother Mary, and Edward Kelly (a packing case maker who lodged with him for 6 months) all gave testimony.
A Benjamin Pilkington corroborated Brown's story. Shee argued that Lindsay was a nuisance, and Conduit had been sent by the neighbours to eject him. The jury took two minutes to return a verdict of not guilty. He was discharged.

7.
THE BABY IN HULME
2 Jul 1890

At 10:20 on a Wednesday evening, Mary Ada Bennett (45) and her young daughter of 45 Fenwick Street, Moss Side were walking along Booth Street, towards Vine Street, Hulme. As she passed the chapel on the corner of Medlock Street she found a black parcel reared against the chapel windows. She touched the package, and her daughter screamed, causing a crowd to form. The parcel seemed to contain flesh, so a policeman was sent for. PC John Faulkner arrived and found the parcel contained a dead child.

He took it to the Cavendish Street mortuary. The outer covering was a black mackintosh which would fit a young teenage girl. The parcel was tied with string. WJ Heslop, a divisional police surgeon, conducted a post-mortem examination, and found the child to be a healthy, well-developed boy. It had either died through exposure or starvation. On July 4th, the inquest was held by deputy city coroner Sydney Smelt at the City Coroner's Court. The jury returned a verdict of wilful murder.

8.
THE WORKHOUSE CHOPPER
30 Jul 1890

William Greenwood (68), an inmate of Withington Workhouse, hit another inmate, John Swindells on the head with a chopper, then partially severing his thumb while they worked in the chiphouse. He was sentenced to a month of hard labour by Mr. Leresche and WW Cooke at the Manchester City Police Court on August 1st, having admitted to *"tapping"* Swindells' head with an axe.

9.
THE ANCOATS INHERITANCE
2 Aug 1890

At about 3:00am on a Sunday morning John Naylor (49), a joiner, savagely kicked, strangled and battered his wife Mary Hannah (45) nearly to death very early on a Sunday morning at their home of 1 New Street, off Pollard Street, Ancoats. He went to their neighbour Ann Grady and asked her to attend to his wife, who was ill through drink. She had some marks on her arm and face and told Grady her husband had beaten her.

Grady sent for PC Evans, who arrived and heard Mary accuse her husband of assault. He said *"What have I done? I have done nothing"*. He was drunk and excited. Evans took Naylor to the Canal Street police station, and was detained on a charge of inflicting bodily harm and committing assault. The same day he was admitted by Inspector Thomas Taylor to Ancoats Hospital with a constable watching him, showing signs of *delirium tremens* (DTs).

At 3:15am Sgt. Wright Whitehead saw her lying on a bed in the kitchen, in great pain with the right side of her neck, face and eye discoloured. She complained of head pains and accused her husband of beating her about the face and head and attempting to strangle her. Her legs were bruised, apparently caused by his kicks. PC Evans was sent to the hospital for a doctor; Dr. Davies attended, and examined her.

He said she was in a critical condition. She was taken to Ancoats Hospital, where from 10:00am Walter Fletcher Boycott, surgical officer, attended to her. She was semi-conscious, breathing heavily and painfully, with a large bruise around her right eye, and some on the upper part of her back and neck. She had contused wounds on her knees and the back of her head was swollen. She was badly congested. At 11:00pm she was dying; by 11:45pm she had died. A post-mortem examination found even more bruises. At the back of her head there was a clot of blood under the scalp, and 20 or 30 bruises. There was extensive meningitis.

He gave the cause of death as minangitis, caused by blows with fists or kicks. Boycott knew Naylor when he was in Ancoats Hospital two years prior suffering burns after falling in a fire while drunk. He was due to appear before the magistrates on August 4th, but was too unwell. A remand was granted.

He had been given £300 upon his father's death two years ago, and as a result was drinking heavily. They were fighting more and more, with fights bothering neighbours. Neighbours acting as peacemakers were 'violently treated'. He, with his neighbours, partly blamed his wife for their fighting; she was 'never stinted' in money by her husband, but often could not satisfactorily account for her purchases. Their only child, Ernest (11 or 12) was clearly badly cared for, despite their house being well-furnished, with a piano.

Police were informed by Alice Lee of 6 New Street that he had assaulted his wife on July 27th. About six weeks before her death she had summoned him for assault, and he was in goal for 14 days. Sydney Smelt, the deputy city coroner, held an inquest on the morning of August 6th, just after Taylor charged him with murder. Her brother John William Hilton (225 Dean Street West, Ashton) identified the body, saying it was 10 months since he had last seen her. Ernest gave testimony stating that his parents had been drinking heavily since July 19th or 26th.

He had seen his mother tumble downstairs when drunk; on July 28th she had landed backwards onto her head. That day there was 'neither fire nor food' at the house, so he hit her in the face, knocking her into the corner, possibly at Mary Ann Shaw's shop at 115 Tame Street, Ancoats. That morning he told Shaw he had withdrawn £20 from the bank to give to his wife. He said that on July 30th his mother got up at about 9:00am, when after half an hour his father kept coming downstairs asking her for food. She said she would go out to get food, but did not, so he hit her breast with his fist. She started to cry and went back to bed. She went out for two hours later but came back without anything. That day Naylor kicked her out of the house, and complained to Lee, who witnessed this, that she never got him any food. On the night of July 31st she sat on the floor in the bedroom and refused to get into bed, so he kicked her twice on the head. He was fairly sober when he kicked her. Mr. Peacock pointed out that he was not wearing shoes when he did this, and a juror pointed out that she should have got him food because he had gone three or four days without, and she had plenty of money for it.

On August 1st she complained she felt ill, and Ernest was sent for Dr. Sutherland of Ancoats Hospital. On August 2nd she became badly drunk and the neighbours made up a bed for her in the kitchen; they told Ernest the doctor had diagnosed drunkenness and bronchitis as the cause of her illness. His father told him Sutherland advised she be taken to hospital, but he refused to let her go.

He said his father was almost constantly drunk and his mother drunk a lot. Shaw said that they often entered her shop; the victim often complained of illness, and Shaw knew it was due to drink. According to her, he would tell her she had enough money to buy food for them and their son, but she rarely did. She had taken the victim in often to protect her from her husband, and had once been hit on the arm while protecting their son.

Walter Fletcher Boycott, resident surgical officer of Ancoats Hospital, said that the death and contusions on her head were due to violence. Thomas Naylor, his brother, said he had had a quarter share of £1700, which he had mortgaged, leaving him £320. Inspector Taylor believed there was £190 left. Catherine Winstanley said that on the morning of August 2nd she was passing the house when she heard the victim moan and cry "Oh! Do not!"

She heard bumps, then Naylor speaking. She knocked on the door and the quarreling stopped. His representative GS Leresche, under the direction of Peacock and Jacques, submitted that there was no case to go to a jury; the evidence was too circumstantial. He also claimed it was only by a majority of one that the coroner's jury returned a manslaughter verdict. The coroner said that however much his wife aggravated him, he had no right to abuse her. W Bratby, one of the judges, said this was not reported in the papers; Leresche said he had been told it. He was committed by the bench for trial at the assizes; bail was allowed.

10.
THE LANDLADY'S SON
9 Aug 1890

Labourer Thomas Cosgrove (34) was sat at the Cheshire Cheese pub on Oswald Street, Ancoats in the taproom, playing dominoes with Hanlon, Brown and James Ashton (21) between 6:45 (when he entered the pub) and 9:00 on a Saturday evening. Ashton's widowed mother Esther owned the pub. Cosgrove told Ashton to get him a quart of beer. When Ashton asked for payment, Cosgrove refused; Ashton said "I will make you", and a fist fight began. Eventually Cosgrove paid and the quarreling ended.

About 15 minutes later, Ashton was stood with his hands in his pockets and back to the fireplace. Cosgrove drew a large clasp knife from his pocket at the beerhouse door and stabbed him in the left breast and the side, saying "Take that, Jim Ashton" or "Jim Ashton, take that". Ashton said "Oh! I am stabbed to the heart! He has knifed me!" and staggered out from the Tame Street door, where he saw his mother returning home.

He said "Mother, I am stabbed; Tommy from Tuam has stabbed me." He fell to the ground bleeding profusely, and was taken on a litter to Ancoats Hospital. He died en route due to the severance of a main artery. Cosgrove immediately ran away, pushing past James Healey of 57 Tame Street, Ancoats, but was tripped up on Every Street by Joseph Horobin, of 8 Richardson's Buildings on Chapel Street, Ancoats, who was in the pub and chased him, and held him down.

PC William Buchanan appeared; Horobin told him Cosgrove had stabbed Jim Ashton. Buchanan took him into custody; Cosgrove never addressed the accusations. The body arrived at Ancoats Hospital at 7:35pm. Walter Fletcher Boycott, resident surgical officer, was handed the bloody knife by PC Hartley. He examined the body and saw a wound in the left breast, and the deceased's clothes saturated with blood. There was a puncture wound between the second and third ribs, two inches below the junction of the left collar bone and breast bone. It was ½" long and 1½" deep. The knife had cut the pulmonary artery. The cause of death was given as "syncope from haemorrhage from a punctured wound in the pulmonary artery".

Boycott saw Cosgrove at the police station with two bleeding wounds on his lower lip. Ralph Brown of 38 Barrington Street, Clayton left the kitchen and went to the passage, hearing Ashton scream and cry "I'm bleeding! Oh, I'm bleeding!" There was a rush of men to the front door, and Brown returned to the kitchen. He went to the taproom as the men were leaving and saw the closed knife on the floor of the passage. He picked it up and gave it to PC Hartley, who was on duty at Pollard Street.

At 7:37pm Cosgrove arrived at Canal Street police station, where Inspector Thomas Taylor claimed he was slightly drunk and excited. While Taylor charged him with stabbing, a telephone message from Pollard Street Fire Station informed them Ashton was dead. He cautioned him, and then let him wash and sleep for two hours. He then charged him with murder. Cosgrove said "I did not do it". He was put back in his cell, and when brought back out for inspection he asked "Mr. Inspector, what do you charge me with?" At 10:10pm Buchanan took him from the cells to charge him with murder; Cosgrove said "they say I've stabbed Jim Ashton. It will be a [damn?] good thing if he's dead."

On August 11th, an inquest in Manchester returned a verdict of wilful murder; Cosgrove claimed that the murder was a drunken accident. He said "It was all through drink, and I did not even remember being taken to the station. I did not intend to kill him". He told the coroner a different story. He told him that he entered the pub at 6:45pm and saw the men playing cards. When the men had finished playing, Cosgrove played another man for a quart of beer; he lost and duly paid. He played another game, and halfway through he went out into the yard. Ashton followed and punched him in the mouth, saying "Are you not going to pay for the quart?" Cosgrove said the game was still on and returned to it. He lost the game and told Ashton to get him a quart, which he paid for. He asked the man he was playing with for another game; Ashton said "You'll play no more here" and punched him in the mouth several times.

That was all he could remember due to being drunk. None of the witnesses recalled seeing another man in the taproom. Esther Ashton said she sometimes would not serve Cosgrove when he was very drunk, and twice when he tried to pay for drinks on trust. He was committed for trial by the coroner's warrant. On the morning of August 12th he was charged with murder at a crowded trial at the Manchester City Police Court. He 'maintained an appearance of solid indifference' during the trial. He was remanded until committed to the Assizes. On November 27th he was sentenced to 15 years penal servitude.

11.
THE RICE PUDDING KILLER
10 Aug 1890

On the night of August 9th, Eliza, the wife of carter Arthur John Corfield, Sr. (25) bought rice from Mrs. Pack on Marsland Street, Ardwick. All of August 10th he stayed in the house except to feed his horses at 5:00pm. That night he allegedly put arsenic in the rice pudding he and their three children were having for dinner at their home of 44 Marsland Street. His wife went to bed and he cleared up. She came down and saw him sitting by the window cleaning his pipe. He said he would not have any more pudding that night, saying there was enough for the children to have warmed up the next day. "It will do warmed up for tomorrow, and what they cannot eat I daresay you can finish."

She said "Yes, I daresay I can." This was unusual for him. He left for work at 5:00am on August 11th. At 1:00pm his wife took the pudding down from a scullery shelf and tasted a little bit of it to test it was cool enough for the children. About 15 minutes after eating it all the children began to vomit and look ill. Eliza fell ill, as did her stepmother and neighbour Harriet Dain, who had tasted it too, assuming the milk was sour.

Dain went home and returned half an hour later saying she was also ill. At 3:00pm Owen Gwatkin, surgeon of Hyde Road, West Gorton was called in to attend to the children. The two youngest, Margaret (3) and Arthur John (nearly 2), had eaten most of it. Arthur died within an hour of Gwatkin's arrival. He asked to see the pudding, and took a teaspoonful of a white powder at the side of the dish for analysis. He also took the pudding. The other child died on August 12th. The eldest, a 5-year-old girl, survived, having only scraped the preparation plate clean; she was still under Gwatkin's care a week later.

Corfield was having an affair with their lodger, an unemployed girl named Mary Eliza "Polly" Fletcher, whom he had met when he worked for John Dyson, a mineral water manufacturer on Temperance Street, Ardwick. Fletcher was a servant there, and their relationship was noticed by other workers and mentioned to Mrs. Dyson. Fletcher was then let go or resigned, and Corfield let her stay at his house, without his wife's permission, for ten days. He left that position June 18th while Fletcher was staying there.

One Saturday Corfield brought Fletcher some vinegar and a cloth to her bed when she was ill with a headache. Following this his wife said Fletcher should go home. He said he would leave the house if Fletcher did. After Fletcher moved out, he began to lose his patience, and they were having words, which was not like them. She then found work with Mrs. Thompson, Corfield's aunt. William Spencer was a lad who worked with Corfield as a lorry boy for John Dyson, a mineral water manufacturer on Temperance Street, Ardwick until Corfield left in July. Fletcher was once a servant there.

On August 12th Spencer and his friend Edward Haddon went to see Corfield at the corn shop where he worked at 7:15pm. According to Spencer, he said "You are a nice fellow, are not you?" Corfield replied, "Why, I know nothing about it". "It looks very black against you". "Yes, it mesmerised me". "How long is it since you saw Fletcher?" "I have not seen her for a few weeks". Haddon said "Why, I saw her on Sunday night, and she said that she had just left you". Corfield went very red in the face and said "If you two will not blab it out I will tell you all about it. The doctors are going to analyse the pudding, and I can tell them before they analyse it what's in it". Spencer said "What was in it?"

"There was arsenic in it. It all happened to be settled in one place instead of being spread about. The wife is stronger than the children and it did not take as much effect on her." Spencer said "It was rather cruel of you to have the little 'un on your knee and be feeding it with the pudding." "I had the little one on my knee because it was very cross with its teeth".

The pair then left to get the tram. That day Gwatkin's assistant Herbert Thompson asked Corfield for the sugar and rice; he called his wife and told her what Thompson needed. She gave him the sugar in a basin and the rice in a packet. On August 14th, the city analyst Charles Estcourt was given a brown paper parcel by the police. The parcel contained two packages, one with sugar and rice and the other with an earthenware dish containing 14 fluid ounces of rice pudding. The sugar and rice were pure, but the rice pudding had arsenic in it. When he poured away the pudding fluid there was 300 grains of heavy white powder left, enough to poison a whole house.

An inquest was held by deputy city coroner Sidney Smelt at the City Coroner's Court on the afternoon of August 15th; Corfield came home at about noon to attend it. He was in the building, but not in the room, and was not called upon. The inquest was adjourned until 5:00pm on August 25th to give police more time to investigate. He knew the arsenic was put in maliciously, but needed to know where it came from and who did it. At 8:00pm on August 15th, Inspector William Leech went to his house with several constables.

They found a white powder "looking like arsenic" in some drawers under a windowsill in the living room. Leech advised him to account for the powder, which was not in a bag. Corfield said "No, I do not know anything about it." He was told he would be taken into custody. He began to cry very hard and kissed his surviving child Lily; his wife said "I have never done anything wrong in my life". He was put in a cab and taken into custody at the Fairfield Street police station as a crowd emerged in the street. Extra police were put on duty to deal with the crowd; even at 10:30pm people were lingering on Marsland Street talking about the incident. The powder was taken from Farfield Street station in an envelope to a druggist who confirmed it to be arsenic.

Leech returned to the house and found more powder in the drawer, and a piece of paper covered in arsenic wedged into a crevice. Corfield further denied any knowledge of it. Superintendent Hartley sent Leech with the powder to Estcourt, whose son tested the powder and confirmed it again to be arsenic. Estcourt kept the arsenic to perform more tests. At 9:30am on August 16th Leech charged him with causing the deaths at Bradford Street station. He replied "I have not done such a thing". That afternoon the children were buried in Philips Park Cemetery, watched by a large and excited crowd.

That day Sgt. Broderick gave Estcourt 3 glass jars respectively containing stomach and contents, intestines and contents, and liver, kidneys and spleens. On August 18th he was brought before the City Police Court on a charge of killing his two children. On August 21st, Leech gathered a sample of arsenic from the Messrs. Kupferberg & Co. works on Collyhurst Road from tubs in the yard. Corfield apparently would go there often; whether he worked there or not is not specified.

On August 22nd, Estcourt received Leech's sample, as well as a packet from Broderick containing arsenic from Bower's Chemical Works at Gorton Brook. Estcourt examined the three packages containing powder from the drawer. The powder in the envelope weighed 420 grains and contained arsenic. 35½% of the powder from the drawers was arsenic; the rest was dust, sand and plaster. The contents of the stomach jar contained arsenic; the others did not.

On the afternoon of August 25th the adjourned inquest resumed at the City Coroner's Court. Estcourt told the court that since August 15th he had received from his son several packets, including two envelopes containing 'dust' from Corfield's working clothes and Sunday clothes pockets from Inspector Hornsby, and another containing the powder from the drawer. There were also two larger packages of powder wrapped in newspaper. Martin O'Rourke (98 Collyhurst Street) was an arsenic acid maker at the Kupferberg works and said he saw Corfield there on August 8th. O'Rourke assumed he was a hawker. Mrs. Bancroft Hothersall (12 Albert Terrace, Longsight), a porter's wife, said she sometimes bought tubs to sell again for washing purposes.

She had known him for two years and sometimes employed him to drive a cart. He and Hothersall had visited the Kupferberg works three times, the last time being July 7th. They would wash their hands after handling the tubs. She sometimes took tubs with arsenic in, but never while he was with her. Her husband told him that arsenic was a dangerous poison, and he would sometimes help to tighten the hoops around the tubs. "She never heard Corfield say that arsenic would make a horse's coat shine".

O'Rourke said he was sure she was with him on August 8th. William Spencer was called upon, and said he did not know much about his relationship with Fletcher. Spencer said Corfield and his wife were on good terms and he would take her and the children to concerts with him. Haddon (16 Buxton Street, Ardwick), also one of Dyson's lorry boys, was also called upon and corroborated Spencer's account; he added that Corfield had said "if it had been sprinkled about the wife would have been done and all". He said he had seen Fletcher and Corfield sat together at Dyson's often but never saw "anything wrong" with them; he never saw them go out together.

Hornsby said Mrs. Corfield wished it to be known her and her husband were peaceable and never really fought. The deputy coroner rejected her request to make another statement because it was unsupportable. He was remanded until September 4th, when he was charged on remand with murdering the two children and attempting to murder his wife and a third child at the Manchester City Police Court. During the evidence Corfield said "As God is my judge, it is not true!" Corfield was described as being sparely built, with a slight moustache and a wisp of beard.

He looked older than he was, and had a prominent nose. Though dressed in his best clothes he had "not made his toilet with any great care". He was not represented by anybody, but on the prosecution's advice he was given a seat in the dock. Estcourt could not attend due to being in London. The prosecution, W Cobbett, feared a remand would be necessary. Martha Christopherson, Mrs. Dyson's sister, told the court that on June 14th she was alone at Dyson's house (118 Higher Ardwick) babysitting.
Fletcher entered at 6:30pm and told Christopherson to leave, which she refused to. Corfield entered at 9:30pm and was in the kitchen with Fletcher until 11:00pm when Mr. Dyson returned home. As Dyson's ostler, Corfield was tasked with taking his horse home. Christopherson said she saw nothing going on between Fletcher and Corfield. On June 15th Christopherson caught the pair sitting side by side in the kitchen with the door shut at about 6:00pm.

They went very red in the face and could not look Christopherson in the eye. Later that evening she saw them coming up the cellar steps, ostensibly to get some coal (despite not having a light with them). Corfield defended himself saying there was a 5-year-old girl in the kitchen with them. He was remanded until September 6th, when he appeared at the Court again. On September 13th he appeared before stipendiary magistrate Francis John Headlam. Emma Hornby, of Kirkmanshulme Lane, Longsight, said she had seen Corfield at Mrs. Annie Adamson's house on that street after Fletcher had become a servant there, a week before the August bank holiday, when Mrs. Adamson and her children were away.

He was in the house for 1½ hour, with his lorry parked outside; then he left, with Fletcher leaving soon after. Michael Connory (193 Clowes Street, Gorton), an agent for the Prudential Insurance Company, said the family were reinsured on March 24th, leaving Corfield entitled to £19 10s. if his wife and children all died. O'Rourke corrected his statement, saying he had not seen Corfield for nearly a month before the incident.

The coroner said O'Rourke's testimony was not entirely reliable, and put it to the court that though Eliza could've poisoned the pudding, she did not have a motive or opportunity like Corfield did. If the charge was one of attempted wife murder, Eliza's statement could be of use, but that was a matter for police to decide when the trial reached the magistrates. Hornsby said the police had intended to get Corfield on that charge.

The coroner agreed, because there were two other people in the house who could've committed the crime and "the criminal might escape". He put a lot of stock in the statements of Spencer and Haddon, whom he believed. The jury returned the verdict that Corfield had wilfully murdered his children. He was committed for trial at the Manchester Assizes, and had nothing to say in his defence. On November 26th he was sentenced to a life of penal servitude after two hours' deliberation at the Assizes, on a charge of attempted murder of his wife.

12.
THE BABY OF TIB STREET
16 Aug 1890

Ernest Vincent (12) found a newly-born girl dead on the doorstep of a warehouse in Short Street off Tib Street, Manchester on a Saturday night. It was wrapped in a parcel of two pieces of rag and brown paper, tied with string. One of the rags was made of women's underwear. He called for PC Perrin, who took it to the Newton Street mortuary.

According to the post-mortem examination by police surgeon Richard Jessop Dearden (174 Oxford Road) the baby was fairly-developed, its skin covered with recent blood and with the space above the bridge of its nose discoloured. The appearance of afterbirth suggested it was less than 24 hours old. Its lungs were healthy. There was effusion under the scalp and a fracture running transversely across from the suture in the forehead to the right and through the parietal bone to the occipital bone.

The parietal bone was divided into two by another perpendicular fracture. The occipital bone was completely smashed in and broken into four pieces. There was effusion of blood on the brain's surface due to the skull's fracture; this was given as the cause of death. On August 19th, the inquest was held by deputy City coroner Sydney Smelt at the City Coroner's Court. A verdict of wilful murder was returned.

13.
THE LONGSIGHT SHOTGUN
4 Oct 1890

William Squirrell (32), a turncock for the Manchester Corporation's water department, shot his wife, Sarah Ann (42), dead on a Saturday at their home of 657 Stockport Road, Longsight. He was described as a sober, respectable man, but for the last 18 months had been quarreling with her; she believed he was seeing a local woman. His children, aged 7, 5 and 2, were in the kitchen when they saw their father return from collecting his wages at the Town Hall at about noon. The eldest, Ben, claimed he took an old double-barrelled shotgun (used for shooting sparrows) off the mantelpiece, put a cartridge in it and shot her at about 12:15.

Two of the children rushed into the street and shouted "Murder!" A nearby labourer named Lear entered the house and saw the victim lying on the couch with her face shockingly mangled. Squirrell lay halfway across her body, moaning heavily, with the gun by his side. Lear said "This is a serious job for you"; Squirrell replied, "Yes, I may as well blow my own brains out now. I will get hung." A crowd had gathered at the door, and a Stockport prison van en route to Strangeways was stopped. The drivers took charge of Squirrell, who made no attempt to explain or deny his crime.

He was given over to the police, and claimed to them he had only aimed the gun at her to frighten her, not knowing it was loaded. A doctor arrived quickly, and announced the death to be instantaneous; the muzzle had been held close to her face, with the shot striking between her upper lip and nose. On each side, terrible gashes poured blood; the nearby cupboard doors were sprayed with blood and brains. He was taken into custody and charged with murder; he said "it is a bad job". He had cartridges in his pockets.

He was brought before the magistrates on October 6th. On October 8th, a coroner's inquest in Longsight returned the verdict of wilful murder. On October 9th, the day before she was given a grand funeral at Philips Park Cemetery, he was charged with wilful murder at the Manchester County Police Court. The evidence given before the coroner was given again, and he was committed for trial at the assizes. He said "you may charge what you like, but it was an accident".

14.
THE HANGING DAUGHTER
21 Oct 1890

Owen Evans (38), a wood machinist and father of 5, came home to 11 Cross Street, Hulme on a Tuesday evening. He found his wife Ellen, drunk, lying asleep on the sofa. She woke up and started to abuse her husband. She took their 8-month-old daughter Ellen off the floor and took a piece of tape about a yard long out of the cupboard. She tied it round the child's neck and left the room, saying "I will make you a witness to this." Evans followed her and watched her hanging the child from the banisters.

He tried to run up the stairs but she kicked him down. She removed the child and began swinging it around on the tape in the kitchen. He wrestled the tape out of her hands and loosened it around the baby's neck. Somehow it survived. The child was taken to Park Place police station, where Inspector Bailey saw a red mark on her neck from the tape. She was tried at the Manchester County Police Court the next afternoon. She was remanded until October 29th, when Francis John Headlam sentenced her to 6 months in gaol with hard labour for assault.

15.
THE HULME AMMONIAC
24 Oct 1890

The wife of Joseph Lester, a carter for Thompson & McKay, put her head on his breast and cried that the neighbours wanted her to turn against him, but she loved him too much to do so. Later that night she was feeling unwell, and sent him to the shop for a few things, including 3d. of brandy, on Friday October 24th. When he got home to 14 Toulson Street, Hulme, his wife was in bed. He took the brandy up to her in a cup. She drank it, and felt her throat burn. It also apparently smelled strange.

She said "Joe, what have you done? You have given me ammonia." "What ammonia?" She ran downstairs and got the ammonia bottle, and brought it back up. She showed him the bottle, which was almost empty. She asked if he had put water in it; he said he had. She poured another cup, and asked if he wanted it. He refused, and she threw it over him. He got up and got dressed.

Her brother was on the sofa downstairs and saw her come down with an ammonia bottle in her hand. She gave him into custody at 1:05am the next morning to PC Robert Hartley, who took him to Park Place station. When charged he said "I did not do it". At 1:30am Hartley brought her to see Dr. WJ Heslop, the police divisional surgeon. She was very excited and kept on accusing her husband. He could not smell ammonia, but could smell strong stale alcohol. Her lips and throat were burnt; the severity differs between articles. He gave her some water and she left.

He appeared at the City Police Court on October 28th on a charge of attempted murder. Mr. Headlam ordered Lester to be discharged, saying his wife had totally imagined the story; her delusional paranoia of her neighbours was testament to this. The case was remanded until October 28th, when he was discharged.

16.
THE WELSH HARP QUARREL
8 Nov 1890

Joseph Cassidy, a carter and Francis Lead, a boatman, were in the Welsh Harp on Lees Street, Ancoats on a Saturday night. They began quarreling, and it came to blows, the first punch being thrown by Cassidy. Cassidy then took off his belt and hit Lead on the eye with the buckle. He pulled a penknife out of his pocket and tried to stab Lead twice, but was stopped by other patrons.

He left the room and returned with a carving knife, which he tried to stab Lead with again, and was again prevented. Lead knocked him down and almost choked him. Cassidy was arrested by PC Marshall, who took him into custody at Canal Street police station. He appeared at the City Police Court on November 10th before H Boddington and W Charlton. He said he was very sorry for what he had done but denied having attacked Lead. He was sentenced to two months with hard labour, which was the severest sentence they could impose.

17.
THE BROTHERS OF ANCOATS
11 Nov 1890

Bachelor brothers Willie (29) and Matthew Hayes (36) went door to door "knocking up" (banging on people's doors to wake them up) between 1:00am and 2:00am on a Monday morning. They had been drinking the night before. John Sandham (5 Cobden Street, Ancoats), another knocker-up, saw them. At 4:45am the brothers left their home of 15 Grime Street, Ancoats for the Houghton Arms on Butler Street there, joined by Sandham at 6:00am. The brothers each had two half-glasses of whisky.

Their widowed mother Mary saw them in the pub at 6:30am; they were slightly drunk and told her they would be home soon. She finished "knocking up" and got home just before 7:00am. Sandham left at 6:40am and went to work at the Bridge Inn on Mill Street, Ancoats. The brothers stayed and had two more halves of liquor each. They left at 7:00am on good terms. Between 9:00am and 9:15am the brothers returned to their home of 15 Grime Street, Ancoats from the pub.

At 9:30am their mother was woken by the sound of quarreling, and shouted "Oh, do not quarrel, you are brothers!" William staggered to the bottom of the stairs and said, "Mother, I am done for", "It is done", or "He's done it", or something to that effect. Matthew fled the scene at about 9:15am. Their mother came downstairs to see him lying on his side on the floor with a chair partly overturned on him. She lifted his head, thinking he had fainted, and then saw his throat had been cut from ear to ear with a razor.

She ran out of the house and screamed. Mary Jane Bailey (175 Mill Street), who had known the brothers for 16 years, was going along Mill Street at about 9:30am and saw Matthew walking coming from Grime Street. She saw a woman running for a doctor, who said something to Bailey. She turned to see the woman when Matthew came up to her and said "I have done it". "What have you done?" "I have cut our Willie's *** throat." Bailey said "Oh! Where are you going?" He did not reply.

Bailey went to the house, and saw Mrs. Hayes in the front room wringing her hands and crying. William was lying on the kitchen floor with the chair on him. She said "Oh, Willie, what's to do?" but he only moved his arm. George Chisholm Winchester, surgeon and assistant to Dr. Quicke, arrived at 9:45am, followed by Dr. Quicke. He observed that the throat was cut from half an inch below the angle of the left jaw to a point two inches behind the right ear. At its deepest it was 2½". William died shortly. News spread quickly and the street was abuzz with commotion. PC Parker heard of the occurrence, and set off in pursuit of Matthew. By 9:20am he had arrived at the Bridge Inn and asked Sandham to buy him another half glass. Sandham told him to wait a bit. "Jack, I have done it." "What have you done?" "I have cut my brother's head off nearly". Sandham went straight to the house to see William on the floor, attended by the two doctors. Matthew went to the Houghton Arms on Butler Street, where he was refused rum due to being so drunk.

He was given a soda water by a barmaid, Harriet Kay, who heard him say "that is the last drink I shall have". He asked for a rag for his cut finger, and said "Our Willie is done for; he's dead". He put his hands above his head and said "my poor brother, my poor mother." He told Mrs. Thompson, the landlady, "that is the last you will see of me". Sandham went from Grime Street to the Bridge Inn, but saw Matthew leaving the Houghton Arms. He shouted "You've done it." "Is he dead?" "Yes, he's dead." 16-year-old Mary Ann Wrigley (75 Bradford Road) was an assistant at William Jackson's pawnshop at 100 Bradford Street.

Matthew pawned his waistcoat there for 9d. at 9:30am. It had some blood on it, which she did not notice. PC Parker had Hayes pointed out to him on Butler Street. He chased him down Hadfield Street and caught him in the doorway of a friend's house on Back Wesley Street, trying to run across the kitchen floor. He handcuffed him; Hayes immediately said, "I know what you want".

He was taken to Canal Street police station, followed by the crowd. While on the way he said "I did it." He asked "Is he dead?" several times. At 10:02am he arrived at the station on a charge of inflicting bodily harm. Sgt. Bates visited the house and found Drs. Quick and Winchester in the kitchen with William, dead. He went back to the station and searched Matthew. The bottom end of an empty razor case was found in his left coat pocket, as well as a knife and sixpence.

The case had contained the razor both brothers used to cut their corns. He was not charged immediately; when he became sober at 2:15 that afternoon he was charged with his brother's murder. He said "I have nothing to say. I would sooner die now." He was badly upset, and later made a statement. The brothers were knockers-up, who would bang on doors around Ancoats to wake people up for work; he was reported as being a mechanic in one article. They were usually friendly when sober, but quarrelled bitterly when drunk. Later that day he was charged at the City Police Court before Francis John Headlam, the stipendiary magistrate. There were a large number of spectators.

He was described as a thick set man with a heavy moustache and keen, penetrating eyes. He appeared dejected, and at one point put his head between his knees and moaned. His mother said the awkward-tempered William was often "naughty" with Matthew, who would tell him "Let mother a-be." According to her, they were inseparable, loving and kind, and drank at the Arms often together.

Inspector Leech requested the trial be remanded until November 12th, but Headlam remanded it until November 15th. The same day, Sidney Smelt, deputy City coroner, opened the inquest. He noted that nobody had actually seen the quarrel or the murder. Smelt asked why Matthew was not present, since he thought it was custom for accused criminals to attend, and thought Matthew had a right to defend himself. Sgt. Bates said that was not always the case. Smelt said he wanted Matthew there, but would deal with the issue in a friendly way rather than clashing with police, which Bates agreed to. He also said something to the effect of "it's not my fault the man is dead", to which Bates said he would relay this to the superintendent.

Smelt said he would talk to the chief constable. Dr. Quicke said the wound was 10" long and had cut the facial, lingual and temporal arteries, and the internal jugular vein. About ½" below the left side of the wound there were two finger-like bruises. The brain contained an unusually large amount of cerum, and the stomach's red patches indicated alcoholism. The heart and liver were slightly fatty. The cause of death was syncope from blood loss. The handkerchief he was wearing had also been cut. Matthew appeared at the Manchester Winter Assizes before Mr. Justice Wills. He pleaded "not guilty" in a firm voice.

The judge said he was Matthew was apparently the better of the two, and their working-class lives led them to the drink, which he held responsible. Sgt. Bates said he never saw them fight in the 10 or 12 years he knew them, but had never seen them when they were drunk. PC Barlow said William had been in custody for being drunk and fighting. He was given 10 years penal servitude for manslaughter. He was released May 11th 1898, and by 1901 was back to living on Butler Street as a knocker up with his family.

18.
THE DEVINE INCIDENT
1 Jan 1891

Around midnight on a Thursday morning, moulder William Henry Carter, his wife Emma (both 28) and her brother Thomas Devine went to Carter's brother's house in Chorlton Street, Collyhurst, where they drank and sang. Devine went home to 49 Montague Street, Collyhurst. At 1:00am, Devine heard Emma return home very drunk. He had seen William on the street sometime before, also drunk. Devine fell asleep on the sofa downstairs. In the bedroom upstairs, the Carters began quarreling. Devine awoke to his sister running downstairs, followed by William.

He wanted her out. She said she would not leave without their child, and William hit her twice in the face. Devine went upstairs to get the child on his sister's request, leaving the Carters sitting close together in the kitchen. She said something offensive about his sister, and he stood up and punched her in the face (it did not appear to be a hard one). She said it again, and then fell forward off her chair, hitting her forehead on the corner of the fender. They picked her up off the floor. She appeared to be fitting, so Carter and Devine sprinkled water on her face.

He went to fetch a neighbour, who was asleep; he knocked on her door for half an hour and returned to see his sister dead. Carter sent Devine for a doctor, and on the way he saw a policeman and reported the incident. Sgt. Pillinger arrested Carter at the house, and was charged by Superintendent Godby at Willert Street police station. Carter said he did not mean to hurt his wife, but admitted he was too drunk to comment.

Carter was charged at the City Police Court later that day, and remanded until January 5th.

On the morning of January 2nd, deputy City coroner Sidney Smelt held an inquest at the City Coroner's Court. Surgeon Joseph Collier, of St. John Street, said his post-mortem examination had found three small contusions on the back of the right forearm, one on the bridge of the nose, and another over her right eyebrow. Both lungs were congested; she suffered heart disease and alcoholism. The surface of the brain showed extensive haemorrhaging, which was given as the cause of death. He suggested it was caused by violence. Carter said "I ca not say anything; we had a few words, and I did strike her".

       The jury returned a verdict of manslaughter, and he was committed for trial. He was indicted for manslaughter at the Manchester Winter Assizes at 11:00am on February 24th, represented by Mr. Cottingham. Dr. Collier appeared and said the diseased state of the victim's brain meant she was likely to black out during times of "mental excitement". He was found not guilty.

19.

THE BABY OF DEANSGATE
1 Jan 1891

Two lads found the body of a newly-born male child behind some hoarding near the railway on Castle Street, Deansgate at 9:00am. They thought the parcel was a football, and one was about to kick it before he noticed the child's head protruding from the black dress material inside the parcel. The next day, an inquest was held at the City Coroner's Court by deputy coroner Sidney Smelt.

Dr. Reynolds of the Manchester Royal Infirmary said the child's face had been "terribly pressed" around the mouth and nose, indicating suffocation. The inquest returned an open verdict.

20.
THE HULME FAMILY BUSINESS
23 Aug 1891

Cabinet maker Harry Wallwork (23) returned home at 10:00pm to 40 Upper Jackson Street, Hulme on a Sunday night, "mad with drink". He worked for his father George, with his brothers James (35) and Alfred, the middle brother. Harry and Alfred worked at the bench, and James was a salesman. George told Harry to go to bed, knowing he was quarrelsome when drunk, but he refused, and sat with Alfred downstairs (Alfred had got in just before Harry, and had had one or two glasses).

He fumbled with his boots. James returned home, very drunk, and went straight upstairs to their bedroom, which was opposite their younger sister Jane's (18) at the top of the house on the third storey. Harry followed him five minutes after. They began talking. Soon after, Jane, who was in her room, heard a bang on the floor. She ran downstairs and got her father, saying "Oh father, there is something wrong". She and Alfred went into the room, which was in darkness before her father lit the gas.

Alfred could see Harry staggering about the room while James was on the floor. Jane thought James had fallen through drunkenness, and then Alfred put his hand on the body and felt a liquid. He slapped Harry's face with this hand, leaving blood on it; he said "Is this blood?" He also might have asked "Have you been striking Jim". His head and breast were leant against the bed, with Harry stooping over the bed.

She said "I am sure something dreadful has happened". Alfred lifted James up; they saw blood on his shirt. There was a five-eighths cabinet maker's chisel on an unfinished dresser by the wall. The chisel had been bought by George on August 20th; tools were usually kept in the cellar, but Jane said she saw other tools in the bedroom.

He had been stabbed in the heart; death was instantaneous, though there was not much blood. George said to another daughter, "Oh, dear, fetch a doctor and a policeman, and Mr. Pearson". He said to Harry "Oh, Harry, what's to do?" Harry replied "What is to do? He's drunk, is not he?" or something to that effect. Jane handed him a chisel; he did not look at it, but told her to take it to her bedroom. Isaac Pearson (46 Upper Jackson Street) arrived at 10:45pm. He saw George stood at the foot of the bed and Harry close to him. He asked Harry "What have you been doing?" "It's all drink, Mr. Pearson; drink's done it." Jane asked if he was dead, and Pearson confirmed it. He then sent for a policeman.

Harry was sobering quickly and crying badly. Dr. Francis Sealey of Dorset Street, Hulme arrived to find James dead. Harry said "Oh, Jim, come back to life", or something to that effect. George, or Sealey, held Harry's hand until the policeman came. PC William Edwards arrived; he knew James from being called in to quiet him several times while drunk. Jane gave him the chisel to inspect. George told him what had happened, and Harry said "I have done it, constable. I am very sorry; it's all through drink". PC George Nash heard a police whistle at 11:05pm. He arrived at the house and saw Harry, drunk, crying bitterly in the kitchen, asking if his brother was dead. He said "I'm the prisoner". Edwards handed him to Nash, and he was arrested; he said "Here I am; I will make no resistance".

Nash claimed he had a small scratch near his left eye and a very bloody lip, which George denied. He put on his clothes and was taken to the Jackson Street police station. Sgt. Dobbs went to the house and removed the chisel. At the station Harry seemed very dejected and sobered up quickly. The neighbourhood was very excited at the incident. At 12:10am on August 24th WJ Heslop (356

Stretford Road), divisional police surgeon, was summoned to Jackson Street police station.

Harry smelled of drink and was recovering from drunkenness. His mouth was swollen, and there was a smear of blood on his left cheek as if hit by a bloody hand. His eyes were swollen from crying and his hands had blood on them. At 8:45am Nash charged him with wilful murder. He replied "I do not remember anything about it; I was drunk". On August 24th, he was brought to the City Police Court before Francis John Headlam, stipendiary magistrate, JF Furniss and Mr. Aronsberg. Harry was described as being a small man with intelligent features, "feeling his position keenly". When Jane was asked if she said anything to Harry when she found James dead, she broke down, crying "Oh, Harry! Harry!"

She told the court that James was a nasty drunk, while Harry was very quiet. She said that on August 23rd, Harry was very drunk at dinner, "nearly mad", and talked a lot with James. She said James was "steady" for the last few months, while Harry was becoming an alcoholic. She said that when their father last went on his holidays, James was constantly drunk; this year George decided not to go on holiday because he knew how much James' drunkenness bothered the family. George said that at dinner, Harry gave James 10s. for cab fare; James had gone out with his girlfriend that afternoon, and the driver knocked at the door asking for payment at 8:00pm. George said "You will get no 10s. off me".

The cabman threatened to sue, and Harry gave him the money saying it was a shame, because James had worked so hard lately. He also said that the chisel had not been in the room before Harry went upstairs, though admitted he rarely went into the room. He said Harry had not seen James since dinner. Alfred said work was being done on the morning of August 22nd in the room that would require the chisel. He maintained there was no quarrel between the brothers, and they seemed friendly. Court Inspector

Drysdale said the evidence was present except for one thing. Sidney Smelt, deputy City Coroner, held an inquest at the City Coroner's Court on August 25th.

Harry was not there because he had been remanded to the gaol by the justices, and getting him to the inquest would cause friction between the authorities; Smelt remarked that it was not his (Smelt's) fault, and regretted Harry's absence. Heslop said the wound was more than 3" deep, and a wound on the forehead indicated he had fallen. The City Police Court completed the trial on August 26th, hearing from Sealey and Heslop. Alfred explained the blood on Harry's face was because he had touched him after touching James' blood.

Jane corrected a mistake in her evidence, and Harry, overwhelmed with grief and speaking low, said he had nothing to say. He was committed for trial at the assizes.

21.
THE ROCHDALE ROAD GANG
12 Sep 1891

On the night of this date, Margaret "Maggie" Waugh (Preston Street, Rochdale Road) was stood with Charles "Charley" Neild on the corner of Livesey Street and Rochdale Road. Joseph Litherland and William Thomas "Tolly" Tollemache soon joined them. A few minutes later, widow Bridget Wilson (40) of 16 Back Preston Street, Rochdale Road, arrived on Livesey Street, alone and apparently looking for someone. Wilson believed they had just come from the nearby scuttling row.

Litherland shouted "Hello, here's our Biddy", and Tollemache put his arm around her neck. According to Waugh, they both fell to the ground. He tried to kiss her, and she fell to the floor. He helped her to her knees, and then pushed her back down. Wilson claimed one man began kicking her, but Martha Abbott (237 Rochdale Road) was stood opposite the men and saw no kicking, and only saw one man do anything. She said she saw Tollemache try to kiss her, and did not mention Tollemache falling. She was taken home by Abbott and her brother once the crowd dispersed; her head was badly hurt. She did not see a doctor.

On September 23rd she admitted herself into the Crumpsall Union Workhouse hospital. She had a neck injury. The staff consulted the police, and she gave a statement. The men were arrested. A city magisterial clerk Mr. Hyde was sent to the hospital to talk with Wilson, who told him she did not think she was going to die. They were brought before the magistrates on September 24th. Wilson was unable to attend so they were remanded, assuming she would be alright in a week. Her condition worsened gradually. She got very bad on September 28th and died on Tuesday, September 29th. They returned to the City Police Court on October 1st, denying any violence; they were "larking about" with the woman in a friendly way and she fell and injured herself.

A coroner's inquest on October 2nd at the City Police Buildings was held by Sidney Smelt, deputy City coroner. The inquest was adjourned until October 5th, when Edward Garvey's testimony was heard; he had seen the men knock Wilson down. Tollemache claimed he tried to take hold of Waugh, but accidentally grabbed Wilson, being "a bit drunk", as (according to him) was Wilson. He claimed she was too heavy to lift and he fell too. He denied saying "hello, Biddy" or kicking her. They were all discharged due to lack of evidence.

22.
THE COLLYHURST FIRE
21 Nov 1891

At 9:00pm on Saturday, November 21st, Mrs. Knott of Back Cropper Street, Collyhurst walked past number 103, and heard singing. At 10:00pm Henry Collings (number 99) heard screams and ran out into the street to see 51-year-old Sarah Brown (of number 103) in flames in a passage entry directly next to the house. He took off his coat and put it round her; with another man they put the flames out. He saw nobody else but Sarah's 17-year-old daughter Mary, a factory hand, running up and down in front of the house crying "Oh dear, oh God!" repeatedly.

Her dress was open at the front, apparently torn. She told the gathering crowd that while her mother was lifting the paraffin lamp from the corner of the mantelpiece she had dropped it and set herself alight. Mrs. Collings had heard quarreling between Sarah and Mary. PC Samuel Jackson was on duty on Oswald Street, Collyhurst when he saw people running towards nearby Back Cropper Street. He followed them, and saw Mrs. Sarah Brown (51) lying in the passage with her clothes on fire.

He pulled off his cape and extinguished the flames, then had her taken to the Royal Infirmary. There was a lot of blood at the entrance to, and on the wall of, the passage. One of Sarah's daughters Sarah Ann (12) came home just after 10:00pm and saw her sister Mary (17), a factory hand, stood at the corner of the street. Mary told her their mother was in hospital with burns and wanted to see her. They went to the Infirmary together, and Mary never mentioned how their mother had been burned. At the hospital, their mother apparently did not speak to them. Nurse Bessie Griffiths claimed that Mary kissed her mother, who said, "Polly, it is too late to kiss me now." Mary replied, "God bless you, Mother."

Jackson returned from the Infirmary and went to Brown's home (103 Back Cropper Street). The table was upside down; there was broken crockery and a broken paraffin lamp on the floor, and a trail of blood led to the passage. In an open cupboard there was some butter; on the butter there was a fragment of a lamp chimney with blood on it. He surmised the lamp had been thrown against a cupboard door.

On their way home, Sarah Ann and Mary met their father William. He asked Mary how Sarah had been burned, to which she replied that "she had caught her mother in flames in the entry". William went to the Infirmary, where his wife told him she had accidentally dropped the lamp.

He had left home early that evening, leaving his wife drunk at home with the lamp was lit on the mantelpiece. When he got home he saw his house in a state of disarray. His daughters said nothing about it. A police sergeant entered, went upstairs and arrested Mary. William told the sergeant he had exceeded his duty by going upstairs, but did not ask why Mary was arrested. At 1:00am on November 22nd the Brown children got home and saw Jackson in their house. He asked what had happened the night before, and Mary gave several statements. Firstly, that as she was going home that night she heard her mother scream, and upon entering the house, saw her on flames. Secondly, that she actually saw her mother on flames at the entry. Thirdly, that she made was that she had had words with her mother, and fourthly, that she had not. She had drunk that night, but very little. He remarked on the oil on the wall and suggested the lamp had been thrown. William said "The neighbours say that it has, but I do not think so."

Later that morning Mary told Sarah Ann: "My mother let the lamp fall when she was lifting it from the corner of the mantelpiece, and it set her skirts on fire". William visited his wife again with his son and Sarah Ann a few hours later. Sarah said she did not blame Mary, and died about midnight on November 22nd.

On November 23rd, Mary appeared at the City Police Court before TH Lowthian and N Bradley. She cried a lot during the trial. Sarah Ann gave testimony. Thomas Palmer, who lived at the back of 103 Back Cropper Street, said he was in his house at the time of the incident, and heard a scuffle that he thought was either a fight or dancing.

Mary was remanded until November 26th. An inquest was held by deputy City coroner Sidney Smelt at the City Coroner's Court on November 25th. Palmer was called again, and Mary and Ann Watson (who lived in the house next to the Brown's, but separated by the passage) corroborated his story, saying they heard Mary's footsteps and a man's footsteps running down the passage.

They claimed Mary had shouted "Mother's on fire. Father threw the lamp. He has done it", and "my father has thrown the lamp at my mother". When she went outside she only saw Sarah, on fire. Thomas Ashton, tenant of the Lancaster Arms on Oldham Road, gave an alibi for William from 8:30pm to 10:55pm. Griffiths was called, and claimed Sarah had repeatedly accused Mary of throwing the lamp at her.

She asked if Sarah had been beating Mary, and she replied that she had told Mary she was too young to go courting, which is why she threw the lamp. She told Griffiths that she did not wish to see Mary get in any trouble. John William Smith, resident surgical officer at the Infirmary, told the court that the cause of death was shock due to extensive burns, syncope from a clot in the pulmonary artery, and acute congestion of lungs from the burns.

She had a cut above her left wrist that had severed a major vein, a bruise on her right temple and another on the back of her head. Her burns covered her breast, face, head, neck and back, and down the shoulders and arms. Her corsets had apparently protected most of her torso. He surmised the lamp had hit her in the chest and the oil had ran down her and splashed over her. Dorothy Fincken, another nurse, said she attended to Sarah that night; she told her "Polly did it" while Mary was in the room.

According to Fincken, Mary told her she was Sarah Ann, and Sarah Ann was Mary. Mary denied this. The jury returned a verdict of manslaughter. She appeared again at the City Police Court before Lowthian and Bradley on November 26th; she was remanded until December 3rd, when she was committed to the Liverpool Assizes on that charge. She appeared at the Assizes on December 7th, before Mr. Justice Lawrance. Mr. Shee prosecuted, and Mary was undefended.

She said "I have nothing to say now, but I am not guilty". The judge urged the jury to consider that someone else had done this; after all, her father had been allegedly heard running down the passage. Without leaving the box, the jury acquitted Mary.

23.
A BETTING MAN FLEES THE SCENE
19 Jan 1892

Sarah Brennan (25) lived with her husband Thomas at 10 Granby Row, London Road. Her husband was a betting man, and was violent with her; he had once thrown a kettle at her, according to their lodger. On December 31st 1891, he returned home from work and saw her with another man in the parlour. Their lodger saw Brennan shout at her, then beat her about the head.

On January 13th she went to her sister's house at 13 Thornton Street, Collyhurst, asking to stay there until her face, which was badly bruise and swollen, was better. Her husband had beaten her, and she swore to her sister she would not return to him. She lived with her sister and was doing well until 2:50pm on a Tuesday afternoon, January 19th. She had eaten a hearty meal, and then suddenly got very ill. Her sister went for a doctor, and returned to find Brennan almost dead. She died at 3:00pm.

On January 20th, a man was shutting up his shop when another man, apparently a stranger, ran up and shoved a letter in his hand, told him to read it, then ran away again. The letter read:
"Dear Tom, I write these few lines hoping you are better off than me. I have not got a friend in the world, and mother has gone away. And, Tom, do not let all the blame on me. Tell them about the man being in the parlour, and about me being good to her, and about her meeting him afterwards, and about you not allowing it in your parlour, and only hitting her with my hands. Tom, do your best for me, and she meet him 8 times. I believe she is lay dead in the police-station."

Sidney Smelt, deputy City coroner, held an inquest on January 21st at the City Coroner's Court. Richard Jessop Dearden, police surgeon, had conducted the post-mortem examination. She had two black eyes and 3 bruises: one on her right cheek in front of her ear, one on her jaw, and one on the back of her head. There was a large effusion of blood extending from the left base of the brain, up the left side and over the left hemisphere.

The death was given as cerebral effusion, likely due to her injuries. A verdict of manslaughter was returned against him. He gave himself in at the Town Hall on the morning of January 22nd, and was taken to the Willett Street station, where he was charged with manslaughter; he said "I did not kill her".

He appeared before the City Police Court on January 23rd before Mr. Furniss and Mr. Kerr. He confessed to beating her on New Years' Eve, and seemed genuinely apologetic. Her sister said she had had to take Mrs. Brennan in 3 times in 2 years due to her husband's violence. Another witness said Mrs. Brennan had admitted cheating on her husband, but said he had cheated on her before, too. He was committed to the assizes, with bail accepted on two payments of £49.

24.
THE PUNCH AT DEANSGATE
8 Feb 1892

Henry Frank Wilson (aged about 60) was a show judge of rabbits and pigeons, and occasionally contributed to papers and magazines. He was about 60, of no fixed abode. On a Saturday night, February 6th, he met young Florence Jones at the Central Station at 9:00pm, and they walked "round the town". Just before 11:00pm they went to the Plasterer's Arms on Gregson Street, Deansgate and had two glasses of ale.

They had a confrontation with James Dolan (lodging at 35 Longworth Street there) while they were there. They left at 11:00pm, followed by Dolan, who hit Jones in the face without provocation. Wilson said "Do not strike a woman like that"; Dolan punched him on the right side of jaw, sending him staggering back and falling into a lamp-post. He fell to the ground, and lay on the flags before becoming unconscious. He bled badly, but nobody helped, apparently terrified by Dolan and his gang.

A woman living on the street, Mrs. Sarah Mather, saw this happen, and said "Oh, you brute!" to Dolan. He replied: "If you split I will put twopennyworth of dynamite under your door and blow you to hell". Due to these threats, the crowd waited a quarter hour before informing police. A constable arrived and took Wilson on a litter to Albert Street station.

His condition worsened, and he was taken to the Infirmary, where he had his stomach pumped. Thinking him to just be drunk, the surgeons advised his return to the station. At 2:00am the next morning Sgt. Grubb saw Wilson mumbling, and drawing his legs up strangely. He told PC Ashton to take him back to the Infirmary, which he did, with two other policemen. Mr. Clegg of the Infirmary (and, later, two assistants) again found there was nothing wrong with him but drunkenness, and the policemen were told to take him back to the station.

That night Wilson's condition grew worse, and very early in the morning a police surgeon recommended he be sent to the Infirmary. A doctor said he had "obvious signs of brain mischief". He was tended to by surgeon Mr. Clegg, who dressed the wound, despite it not bleeding especially. After about an hour he deemed Wilson to be drunk. He died from brain laceration at 3:30am on Monday, February 8th, having never regained consciousness. Dolan was arrested on the night of February 7th by PCs Ashton and Burgess. When he was charged with manslaughter he said nothing. He appeared at the City Police Court on February 8th; the police successfully applied for a remand until February 11th.

Sidney Smelt, deputy City coroner, held an inquest on the morning of February 10th at the City Coroner's Court. Richard Jessop Dearden, police surgeon, had conducted the post-mortem examination. He found that the skull fracture was not noticeable by touch or sight without looking inside the skull. The jury returned a verdict of manslaughter against Dolan. The foreman expressed the opinion that the Infirmary staff should have investigated more, and advised the Infirmary Board to consider the case. Smelt promised to talk with the authorities at the Infirmary. He reappeared before the magistrates on February 11th, and called upon a Mary Haggerty (6 Byrom Street, Deansgate), who was with Dolan, or a female friend, in the beerhouse at the time.

She said she had seen Jones hit Dolan 3 times in the face, because Dolan had reprimanded Wilson for using bad language. Wilson (who was "treating" her), causing the landlord to remove them. She said Dolan stayed in the beerhouse. He was committed for trial at the Assizes at Strangeways on March 16th before Mr. Justice Collins, on a charge of causing death. He was defended by Charles Pilling McKeand, while Mr. Foard prosecuted. JA Ratcliffe, the landlord of the Plasterer's Arms, gave testimony, saying he had thrown all of the people involved out after their confrontation in the pub. McKeand said the blow was given in hot blood, but not with vindictiveness. The judge said nothing had been done to justify Dolan hitting Wilson that hard; he showered praise on PC Backley, who insisted Wilson be taken to the Infirmary. He criticised the Infirmary staff, but hoped it was just a mistake due to the high volume of drunks the Infirmary actually get. Surgeons Clegg and Dearden both testified that nothing could have been done to prolong Wilson's life after the incident.

McKeand mentioned that Dolan had been given 2 medals from the Royal Humane Society for saving life in 1881 and 1886. The judge ruled that the punch was brutal and unprovoked, and had caused Wilson's death. Taking into account his apparent usual good behaviour, he sentenced Dolan to 12 months' hard labour in prison for manslaughter.

25.
THE BABY IN THE PEGGY TUB
18 Apr 1892

Robert Armstrong was a labourer, living at 12 Back Clowes Street, Chorlton-on-Medlock. He left for work at 7:20am on a Monday morning, leaving his 12-month-old daughter Ada and his wife at home. His wife, Lizzie (27) had been unwell for about a fortnight, apparently broken-hearted and refusing to sleep or eat. At 8:30am, Emma Greaves (9 Hughes Street, Chorlton-on-Medlock) called on Mrs. Armstrong, her sister. She was half-dressed. Greaves asked "Are you coming down to our house today?" "Yes."

At 9:05am she came to his workplace in Ardwick. He said "What do you want with me?" "I have drowned our Ada." "Lizzie, is it true?" "You will find it out by and by." He put on his coat and went home with her. As they walked home, she said "You had better get a policeman and give me in charge". She repeatedly said "I have drowned our little Ada" and nothing else. At some point she gave him the door key.

At 9:25am they saw Sgt. James Smith and PC Jackson on Downing Street. They gave a statement; Jackson arrested Mrs. Armstrong on suspicion, and the four went to the house. In the kitchen they saw the small peggy tub with a board on top of it. They took the board off and saw Ada drowned in 8" of water. She appeared to have been pushed down, lying horizontally near the surface. Smith asked Mrs. Armstrong what it was; she had no response, and was apparently in a "stupid condition".

He removed the child, and took Mrs. Armstrong into custody. She said nothing in her defence, but took her purse from her pocket and gave it to him. At 10:00am police surgeon WJ Heslop saw her at the Cavendish Street police station. He examined her for some time and concluded she was suffering from melancholia. He asked her why she killed her child; she claimed something forced her to, and she could not help it.

Sidney Smelt, deputy City coroner, held an inquest on the morning of April 20th at the City Coroner's Court. Armstrong said his wife had been in Prestwich Asylum before they were married in 1887, and he did not know why she was sad lately. Smelt suggested the murder was because Armstrong drank, and this angered his wife. He said he did not drink much; he had been drinking on April 19th, but was not drunk. He said he had not slept in the house since the murder.

He admitted he drank on April 14th after getting his wages; he had had two pints. Smelt asked if that irritated his wife, which it did not, because he gave her his wages. "Have you been drinking this morning?" "I have had two or three glasses of beer." "Then you ought to be ashamed of yourself." "Ashamed of myself?!" "Yes." "I ca not help it Sir, I am not a teetotaller. I can not sleep in the house."

"I am sorry for you, as I am for anyone in trouble. It is all very well to make this an excuse for drinking. You have been drinking because you are fond of it. A man does not drink because he is in trouble, but because he is fond of drink. You remember the lines of Browning: You have met a friend or else you are dry, or else you may be by and by, or any other reason why".

Armstrong said he had never missed work due to drunkenness, and Smelt replied:
"He ought to have kept his senses clear to come here. He comes here at 10 o'clock this morning, and has been drinking already".

Greaves attested to her sisters' mental illness, claiming she had been in the Asylum for 9 months in about 1885 for jumping into the canal near Brook Street. Smelt asked whether she knew that her sister had been before the magistrates 8 or 9 times; she did not, and neither did Robert, but he did know she had appeared at least once in the past. WJ Heslop, who conducted the post-mortem examination at Cavendish Street station, said the death was due to suffocation from drowning, and there were no signs of violence on the body.

A verdict of wilful murder was returned against Mrs. Armstrong. A juror asked whether the jury could include insanity in their verdict, and another said there was not enough evidence to justify an insanity plea. The coroner advised they send the course to be investigated before a judge at the assizes, and that it was not their job to decide the sanity of the accused, but rather to ascertain a cause of death. The witnesses were bound over to give evidence at the assizes.

She appeared at the Manchester Crown Court on May 18th before Mr. Justice Collins; Mr. Yates prosecuted and Mr. Sparrow defended her. Evidence from 2 prison doctors and a Home Secretary medic all agreed with Heslop's diagnosis of melancholia, and said she genuinely did not know the difference between right and wrong. Sparrow said the jury should return a special verdict to account for her inability to control her actions at the time. She was detained at her Majesty's pleasure under treatment, under the condition she would be freed if she ever recovered.

26.
THE CANAL STREET SCUTTLE
23 Apr 1892

Around April 16th, James Hands (6 Duke Street, Ancoats), a 16-year-old dyer's labourer, heard that there was to be a scuttling fight between two gangs. One gang, the Bradford Street lads, included 16-year-olds cooper William "Billy" Willan, Edward Fleming and Charles Davidson, and probably Durkin, Thomas Riley (18, a vase hawker of 42 Hanover Street) and James Walsh (18, of Coal Street, Ancoats); the other, Limer Street lads, included Peter Kennedy (58 Addington Street, Ancoats), a 16-year-old dyeworks labourer at Crabtree's, Ancoats. Around 5:40pm on April 21st, Hands, Willan, Fleming and Davidson were walking home from work when they met Kennedy.

Willan asked, "Is this scuttle over?" Kennedy replied, "What scuttle?" "Why, with these lads here." Willan pointed to some other lads Kennedy was with. Kennedy said "I know nothing about it", and they left him. They planned to "dose" (hurt) him the next night. Around 5:40pm on April 22nd, Hands and Fleming saw Willan and Davidson in an entry that they knew Kennedy would walk down. There were lots of broken pop bottles on the floor. Willan said "Get some pop bottles and have a smack at Kennedy". Kennedy saw them and ran; they chased him over a stepbridge off nearby Union Street. Willan said "Let's meet him tomorrow at dinner and dose him then", and they all agreed.

On Saturday morning, April 23rd, Willan, Fleming and others saw Kennedy and his friends on their walk to work. Kennedy asked "What is it going to be?"

Fleming answered, "Nothing, if you will let me go to my work."

Kennedy and his friends walked off, followed by Willan's lot. Kennedy said, "Lash out behind!" and saw them get their belts out. He tried to run away, but fell; just before the belts landed, he scrambled to his feet and fled. Fleming said all he did was ask Kennedy to drop the scuttle so he could get to work. He admitted he had a stick in his hand, but that was just because another lad had asked him to hold it while he went to buy tobacco.

About 12:40pm that afternoon, Hands met Fleming, Willan and Davidson on the corner of John Street. He told them Kennedy would not get paid until 1:00pm. They all went to the corner of Mill Street and Great Ancoats Street. Kennedy, James Cowen (19, of 5 McGee's Buildings on Primrose Street, Ancoats), James "Jimmy" Meehan and John Carr (17, of Ludgate Street, Rochdale Road) passed the lads at 1:30pm on their walk home from work. The lads followed Kennedy down to the top of Cannel Street, where Hands turned to go home, apparently because he had to, not because he morally objected to the affair. Willan opened a narrow-bladed knife, said "I am going to dose him with this", and replaced the knife, open.
Willan and Fleming were then joined by about a dozen others, including Metcalfe, Durkin, Riley and Walsh, who surrounded the pair, holding belts and sticks. Davidson apparently then arrived, and Willan gave him his belt, showing him the knife. Kennedy overtook them, and Davidson asked Willan "What is it to be?" "Whatever you like."

Kennedy began to run, but only made it 2 yards before Willan pulled out the knife and stabbed him in the left side from behind. Willan fell on his hands and knees, while Kennedy ran away, crying "Oh!". Davidson rushed at Meehan with a belt, but he managed to escape. A cry of "Police!" went up, and Davidson ran away. Kennedy and Carr walked to the Royal Infirmary, and arrived in a state of collapse. He was attended to by John William

Smith, resident surgical officer. Hands was caught up by William near the New Islington Baths. He said "Will you take my wages home and mind the knife?".

Hands obliged, and Willan wiped some blood off it. He said "I have dosed Kennedy". "Whereabouts have you dosed him, in the head?" "No, in the ribs" He also said "If you get copped, do not round on me", or "I have given him fat, do not round on me". Riley, Walsh and Durkin met Willan later that afternoon in Wharf Street, where Willan told them he had stabbed Kennedy. Kennedy died at 8:00pm on May 8th.

Following the taking of Kennedy's depositions, Willan was taken by Sgt. Wright Whitehead into custody at Fairfield Street station on April 25th. He said "I did not do it. I received a knife from Edward Fleming, which I gave to James Hand in Cannel Street". Fleming was taken into custody that evening, and admitted hitting Kennedy with a stick. He said "The others did as much as we did". Fleming and Willan were brought before EM Henriques and a Mr. Holt at the City Police Court on April 26th. Because Kennedy was in hospital and unable to attend, Fleming and Willan were remanded, and the witnesses were bound over to attend at the Assizes. On April 27th Davidson was arrested. They appeared again before Henriques and Holt at the City Police Court on April 29th. Kennedy died May 8th. An inquest was held by deputy City coroner Sidney Smelt on May 11th. Kennedy's father Thomas gave evidence of identification, and said he had visited his son in hospital; he had told him Willan had stabbed him.

Hands told the court that the scuttling fight had begun partly due to rumours that a Limer Street lad had been hitting girls, or as Davidson put it, "banging some girls". The gang war had been going on for about 5 or 6 weeks. Another rumour, not heard by Hands, claimed that Kennedy had stopped Fleming from bullying a small boy. Davidson, cautioned, gave a statement, as did Willan, who claimed he had been attacked by Limer Street lads earlier that week, Kennedy being one of his assailants. He also claimed that on April 21st, when he asked Kennedy if the scuttling was finished, he had responded: "we will talk about scuttling when I have put two or three in the infirmary", and that a friend of his was attacked by Limer Street lads on the night of April 22nd.

When the Court adjourned for lunch, Smelt said he wanted all 8 or 9 scuttlers before him. Dr. John William Smith was then called. Smelt remanded Fleming, Davidson and Willan until May 12th to give the police an opportunity to gain additional witnesses. That same day they appeared on remand before C. Lister and other magistrates at the City Police Court; they were remanded on Sgt. Whitehead's application pending the Coroner's inquest.

The inquest of May 12th saw Carr give a statement that he was walking about ten yards in front of Kennedy, and saw Willan, Hands, Fleming and Davidson "peeping into" Great Ancoats Street. There were several others behind them, whom he believed to be part of their gang. He heard a shout, turned around and saw Kennedy running across Great Ancoats Street, shouting "I'm stabbed!" He had heard that "some lads were going to be onto Kennedy". He asked Kennedy who stabbed him, and he told him he did not know. He moved Kennedy's hand away to see him bleeding, and then helped him to the Infirmary.

Hawker George Metcalfe (19, of 8 Coates Street, Ancoats) said he was on the corner of Mill Street with the accused at the time of the attack. He had met them on his way to gamble on Allum Street (off Great Ancoats Street, parallel to and west of Cannel Street), and heard Willan and Fleming say they were going to dose Kennedy. He told the coroner that he was not interested in being part of the dosing and generally did not associate with those lads. He said that he saw Davidson holding a belt above his head, and Fleming chasing Kennedy with a stick.

Willan stabbed Kennedy at the corner of Allum Street. Kennedy had his hands up, backing away from Willan with a frightened expression. They were face-to-face, and Willan held the knife in his right hand when he stabbed him.

Walsh said he was going along Ancoats Lane when he met Willan's lot at the corner of Mill Street. He asked them what was going on, and Willan said "there's a bit of bother on". Willan showed him the knife. He saw Fleming holding a short stick with a knob on, but did not see Davidson holding anything. He walked behind them by 40 or 50 yards, but came close to them near the end of Allum Street. He saw Willan hold the knife in his left hand, with Kennedy's back to him. He said Fleming ran behind Kennedy, but did not use the stick. Davidson, brandishing a belt, chased another lad into a clothes shop.

Edward Armstrong (6 Ludd Street, Ludgate Hill), a younger boy, said he saw Davidson chasing Meehan with a belt, just after Kennedy was stabbed.

Patrick Mannion (14, of 94 Pump Street, Rochdale Road) said he saw Kennedy running across the road shouting "I'm stabbed", with Fleming holding a stick. He told the coroner he had resigned from the works that he was employed at, because he was afraid of being in the area after what happened to Kennedy.

Whitehead produced Kennedy's depositions, which read: "About 1:30 on Saturday I was at the corner of John Street, Great Ancoats Street. I felt a stab in the left side, and it was from behind. I did not see who did it. I ran away, and they followed me with their belts. A boy named Fleming was there with a stick in his hand. When I was stabbed I saw Willan, and said "What do you mean?" and he ran away with the other lads. I never had a quarrel with him. I saw nothing in his hands but the stick." When cross-examined by Willan, he said "I could not say you stabbed me. I do not remember seeing a youth hit with a belt on Sunday night before. I heard after about it."

The Coroner said that the evidence was satisfactory in showing Willan stabbed Kennedy. Though a clear motive was not obvious, there was enough evidence to show why he died. He urged that co-conspirators to the murder be included in the verdict, and as such the jury returned a verdict of wilful murder against Davidson, Fleming and Willan. They censured Hands for doing nothing to prevent the murder, despite knowing of it.
On the afternoon of May 12th, the three appeared before Henriques and Mr. Lomax at the City Police Court, and were committed for trial at the assizes for wilful murder. They appeared at the Manchester Spring Assizes on May 20th.

HW West, Q.C. and Mr. Scott prosecuted, while Willan and Fleming were defended by Charles Pilling McKeand; Davidson was defended by Mr. Mellor. West said the case was about scuttling, and he could not see any difference in guilt between the three accused. He told the story, saying that Willan had a knife, Fleming a belt, and Davidson a stick. The knife cost Willan 2d.. He said stabbing Kennedy in the back was a dastardly and cowardly act. Willan was sentenced to death, while the others were acquitted.

27.
THE AXE AT ANCOATS
6 May 1892

Shoemaker Patrick McCabe (35) hit his wife Bridget several times on the head with an axe on a Friday afternoon at their home of 3 Garrick Street, Ancoats. He handed himself in at Cannel Street Station, and told Inspector Bates to go to his house, as he had been "thumping" his wife. His hands were covered in blood, so Bates asked him what he had been thumping her with. "With an axe." A constable went to the house and found her bleeding from two wounds on her head that had penetrated her skull, the kitchen drenched in blood. She was taken to Ancoats Hospital in a dangerous state, and her depositions were taken. He was charged with assault, and said he did not know what he was doing, and that he was drunk at the time.

He appeared before Mr. Kerr and Mr. McDougal at the City Police Court the next day, on a charge of attempted murder. He said his wife had tried to poison him. He was remanded, and appeared before C Lister and Mr. Lomax on May 13th at the same Court. He appeared at the Manchester Summer Assizes before Mr. Justice Vaughan Williams on July 16th. JM Yates prosecuted, and Mr. Cottingham defended him. James Henry Williams, resident surgeon at Ancoats Hospital, said Mrs. McCabe's head was fractured in four places, with 16 wounds in her scalp. The trepanning operation had to be done twice. He said she was just about out of danger at the time of the trial.

The defence stated that he was suffering from mania, caused by drink and aggravated by a recent fall injurious to his brain; however, it was proven that he was sane when he was admitted to the gaol, and was no longer an insomniac (if, indeed, he ever was). The judge said the issue was whether McCabe knew what he was doing when he committed the crime, and not how insane he was at the time of the trial. The jury returned a verdict of guilty, though some jurors recommended mercy. The judge said he agreed with the verdict, but would defer passing sentence while considering the recommendation of the jury. He was sentenced to 10 years' penal servitude on July 16th.

28.
THE WORKHOUSE BABY DROWNED
10 Jun 1892

Clara Schofield (23) left Withington Workhouse with her two-week-old baby on the evening of June 8th. On June 9th a Mrs. Finnerty (Rathbone Street, Chorlton-on-Medlock) took her in and let her stay the night. She went to bed, locking the doors and taking the keys upstairs, leaving the Schofields lying on the sofa in the kitchen. When she came downstairs the next morning, Schofield was there, but not the baby. She asked where it was, and was told that she had given the baby, through a window, to a woman who promised to adopt it. She asked that Schofield take her to the house, but she refused, saying "it is my baby, and I can do as I like with it". Schofield kicked her out, and she was taken in by neighbours who then called the police.

PC Samuel Jackson arrived and searched Finnerty's house, but could not find the child; he took her into custody. She appeared before Mr. Furniss and Mr. Parlane at the City Police Court on June 11th. She was remanded for a week pending further investigations. The baby was found by two nightsoilmen, dead on June 13th in a sanitary can at Water Street Depot, having been taken from Rosamond Court, near Rathbone Street. When Jackson charged her with the death, she said "I did nothing to the child".

Sidney Smelt, deputy City coroner, held an inquest at the City Coroner's Court on June 15th. There was "a long list of witnesses called". As Schofield was in Strangeways at the time, it was hard to gain identification; a female officer at Withington Hospital was called upon; she said Schofield had left the hospital with the baby wearing the same clothes it was found dead in. She could not identify the baby, however, so a nurse was called upon, who said the baby bore a resemblance to the one she saw in the hospital.

Finnerty was called upon, and said the clothes the baby was found in were "the very ones" worn when they arrived at her house. When Smelt asked how she knew this, however, she seemed less certain, saying "well, they are like them". Her husband Michael said he saw the Schofields downstairs at 4:00am on June 10th. Mary Ann Brett, a neighbour, said she saw Schofield at 6:00am, with a folded newspaper in her hand.

The Finnerty's lodger, Ms. Mooney, said she talked to Schofield later that day. Schofield had said she had been to see the baby at a house near the Clarendon Hotel on Clarendon Street, where its carer had "promised to do well by it". WJ Heslop, police surgeon, said he had examined the baby, and found it had a slight bruise under the right temple that was more extensive under the scalp. The cause of death was given as suffocation, and he was told by PC Lowing that its clothing was found over its face. A verdict of wilful murder was returned.

She was found guilty of wilful murder by Francis John Headlam at the City Police Court on June 17th.

29.
THE RUSHOLME SPUD
19 Jul 1892

At 7:00pm a Monday night, July 18th, Frederick Davies (11), son of a widow, and a joiner's son, Norman Nuttall (5), of 62 and 26 Rusholme Grove, Rusholme respectively, were playing out. At 7:30pm Nuttall ran back home screaming, and met his mother outside the house. He told her Davies had thrown something (a potato) at him on Dyson's Square. There was a wound just over his left ear. His mother, thinking it was not serious, tied a handkerchief around his head and put him to bed. He became seriously ill in the morning of July 19th, and lost consciousness.

Dr. Waddell was called in, but Nuttall's condition deteriorated until his death that afternoon. Sidney Smelt, deputy City coroner, held an inquest at the City Coroner's Court on July 20th, and formally committed Davies for trial on a charge of manslaughter. He said he did not intend to hit Nuttall; he wanted to hit the wall behind him to frighten him "and make him give over calling him names". Another boy, Stanley Lambert, corroborated this story. WJ Heslop, police surgeon, conducted the post-mortem examination, and found that Nuttall had died from a skull fracture, more likely incurred by a rock than a potato. Davies' mother was overcome when she heard the jury's verdict.

Smelt said he would take the same bail as the magistrates if Davies returned for his trial. Davies appeared before Mr Elliott, W Murray and TT Shann at the City Police Court on July 21st. Davies was represented by John William Addleshaw, Jr., of Addleshaw & Warburton. The Chairman called the death a pure accident, and the boys were on good terms when it happened. The bench decided Davies had been punished enough, and he was recommended to be discharged.

He appeared at the Manchester Assizes before Mr. Justice Bruce on November 25th. Mr. Cottingham prosecuted, while Mr. Overend Evans defended Davies. The judge asked Cottingham if there was any real point in carrying on with the case.

The bench agreed that prosecuting a boy of 11 for manslaughter seemed rather harsh, even if he had committed the crime. Cottingham was glad to have his "most unpleasant duty" relieved. Mrs. Davies said the case was one of boys will be boys, but said that throwing rocks is a public mischief and she would forbid her son from doing it in future, as per the judge's advice.

30.
THE IRRITATED NEIGHBOUR
3 Sep 1892

Catherine Kitts (42) lived with her 17-year-old daughter and two younger sons at 3 Mannion's Buildings on Abbot Street, Collyhurst. She was widowed in 1890 from a gasworks accident, and since then had supported herself and her children single-handedly. She lived next door to Mrs. Moore and her married son. Mrs. Moore had another son Michael (28), a plasterer and old soldier lodging on Old Hall Road, Middleton. Michael often visited his family, and became acquainted with Kitts' daughter, Mary Winifred. On the afternoon of Saturday, September 3rd, Moore came to Manchester and got on the spree to his brother's house.

Mary left for the theatre at 6:50pm; Kitts was drinking with two other women, but was quite sober. Moore arrived at the house about 10:00pm with Thomas Kelly (13 Alfred Street), whom he had invited in for beer. Moores had a lot of liquor at home, but left for more beer. Between 10:00pm and 11:00pm Mrs. Kitts left the house to look for her daughter, whom she believed was at Moore's house. She was drunk.

She entered the house and sat on Kelly's lap, telling him he was her best friend since her husband's death. Mrs. Moore claims she asked him for a kiss, but Kelly denies this happened. Moore came home, also drunk, and ordered her out. She refused, and a fight ensued, with him pushing her into the yard. Her foot became entangled in a bag; she fell on her face against the doorpost. She returned home, and Mrs. Moore locked the door to stop her son following her. Kitts came back a few minutes later and threw a saucer through a window, saying that if Moores did not open the door, she would open the windows.

Moores went outside and began hitting her in the face, then followed her into her house. His mother saw this, and ran back to her house to tell her daughter-in-law Alice to get Kitts away. She did not go, but Moore returned a minute or two later. She did not see Moore kick or knock Kitts down.

Mrs. Young (4 Mannion's Buildings) had been talking with Kitts just a few minutes earlier. She saw Moore at the door of his brother's house; she questioned him, and he said something obscene and threatened to serve her the same way. A crowd gathered, and Moore was pulled into his house by his relatives. Messengers were sent to one or two doctors' houses, but none could be found.

Ann Bowler, a neighbour, heard screams and breaking glass, and ran into the house to see Moores kicking and punching Kitts' head in on the kitchen floor. She said "Moore, do not do that!", but to no avail. She ran out screaming "Murder! Is there no-one that will save a poor widow woman?", and pleaded with Mrs. Moore to get her son away.

PC Wilshaw attended some minutes later. He saw Kitts on the kitchen floor unconscious, lying in a pool of her own blood. Her face was almost unrecognisable, and there were blood marks all over the kitchen.

Wilshaw and PC Wilson took him into custody at the Willert Street station. Mary got home at 10:30pm to find her mother dying on the sofa, surrounded by people. In the meantime, Kitts was taken to the Royal Infirmary, where house surgeon John William Smith declared she had died en route. She had 19 bruises on her arms and above. There was an irregular wound ½" long on the back of her head. The cause of death was given as haemorrhage from internal and external wounds. He said all of the wounds could have been caused by kicks. Moore was brought before the stipendiary magistrate on the morning of September 5th.

Later that day the coroner opened an inquest, and returned a verdict of manslaughter. He reappeared at the City Police Court before TT Shann, J Parlane and R Hall on September 6th. Kelly told the court that while he was at the house, Mrs. Kitts had sat on his knee and told him he was her best friend since her husband's death; Moore told her to leave, and she obliged. Moore's mother Mary said that when Kitts was asked to leave she said "No, you swine, I will not go out for you. When you get a house of your own you can order me out".

Moore claimed that when he left the house it was to return to Middleton. He then saw her preparing to throw another saucer. He hit her, and she called him an offensive name, so he prepared to hit again. She struck at him with a poker, then hit him twice. He pushed her, and she fell near the fireplace; he thought her face had hit the oven door. He then ran away.

The inquest evidence was repeated, and he was committed for trial at the assizes on the capital charge. He was tried on November 26th before the Honourable Sir G Bruce at the Manchester Assizes. He was defended by Charles Pilling McKeand, while CH Hopwood, Q.C., M.P., and Mr. Aitken prosecuted. He was sentenced to 5 years penal servitude for manslaughter. He was released from Portland on October 6th 1896, a year early.

31.
THE PARCEL IN THE CANAL
13 Sep 1892

At 10:30pm on a Wednesday night, a woman named Alice Farrar (Whalley Street, Newton Heath) left her house to go to a public house to check the time. While crossing Royle's Bridge on Whalley Street she saw registered midwife Mary Ann Hall (53, of 59 Ridgway Street, Ancoats) come up behind her. She went on to the pub, and on her way back saw the woman was still there; Farrar's husband William, a painter and paperhanger, was at the other end of the bridge. They saw her take a white parcel from under her arm and throw it up towards the bridge wall.

Alice moved towards Hall, and the parcel fell backwards at her feet. Hall then ran away; Farrar shouted "Bill, follow that woman, for I am sure it was a child". She picked the parcel up, opened it, and found the decomposed body of a female infant. William caught up to Hall a short distance on, and told her she was wanted on the bridge. She said "You are mistaken, it is not me".

They returned to the bridge, where Henry Hulme (50 Violet Street, Beswick) had wrapped the baby in a piece of paper. Hall said "Where is it?", and Hulme said "It is here", putting the baby in her arms. Hall passed Farrar on the bridge, who put the child in her arms. He saw his wife coming home over the bridge; Hall was between them.

She immediately contacted police and gave a statement. PC George Chesters arrested Hall on the bridge, who said "I am innocent". Sgt. George Gibbons searched her house while her sister and daughter were there. He went into the cellar, which smelled so badly that he had to take out the window to let air in. On the cellar floor there were 4 old buckets of lime, and jars containing medicine and chemicals. He did not finish his search of the cellar, and intended to take the floor up. The back bedroom and front room (the latter being where Mrs. Hall and her sister slept), both had 3 beds and mattresses on one bedstead. He also found a number of medicine bottles, powders and pill boxes, some empty.

Hall told him this was because other young ladies sometimes lived there. A portmanteau in the house contained blood marks that ostensibly resembled the limbs of a young child. One compartment contained a rag containing matter; another contained some pawn tickets, and the lock appeared to have been used aggressively. He took it to Hall at Cannel Street station; she said she had bought it from a pawnbroker in Butler Street, Ancoats. When he showed her the blood stain, she hesitated, and then said "Oh, I think I recollect what has caused it. I was at the Isle of Man about two years ago, and I brought two chickens back with me". He showed her the broken hinge, and she said "I have the key in my pocket". He asked why she had had to force it open if she had the key, and she made no reply.

She appeared at the City Police Court on September 16th before R Hall and Cllr. Roberts. The police applied for a remand in order to investigate further; she was remanded for a week. The same day, Sidney Smelt, deputy City coroner, held an inquest at the city Coroner's court. William Farrar told the court that Farrar had left the house with another woman that night; upon hearing this he ordered William out of the court, and got Alice in, who said she did not walk with another woman; a neighbour had just called in to say "goodnight".

William was called back in, and continued his evidence. Hall claimed the blood in the portmanteau was chicken blood from Whitsuntide, but Gibbons remarked that it smelt like a decomposed body. Richard Jessop Dearden (174 Oxford Road), divisional police surgeon, said he had performed the post-mortem. The body was of a poorly-developed 4lb. baby girl, about 4 days old. Her parietal bones were fractured, but there was no suffusion of blood, suggesting the fractures were caused after death.

The cause of death was given as either inanition or starvation. Hall said the baby was not hers and knew nothing about it. Smelt said the jury would find it difficult to decide if the death was murder or manslaughter. He did not see the point in adjournment, and said the only evidence to send Hall to trial would be to find the baby's parent. He said if the police found any more evidence, they could send her to the magistrates. The jury returned a verdict of "found dead".

That afternoon, Gibbons directed some men to take up flags in the cellar. The ground under the flags was very hard, indicating it had been undisturbed during Hall's tenancy there; she and her husband had stayed there a few months, having lived in the area before then. The front room on the ground floor resembled a surgery, with rows of small drawers containing phials and bottles lining two sides of the room. Some of the bottles and phials were empty, and the whole room looked untidy and neglected. She told police she purchased the goods at auction. The house was surrounded all afternoon by female neighbours gossiping.

On September 23rd, Hall was charged before Francis John Headlam at the City Police Court with attempting to dispose of a body. Gibbons was called upon, and said he had discovered that a cab with a woman inside drove up to Hall's house on September 8th. Hall, represented by Mr. Sims, reserved her defence and was committed to the assizes for trial, bail allowed. She was bailed on September 28th.

On September 30th she appeared before the Crown Court on a charge of public nuisance through disposing a body on a highway. Prosecuting was Overend Evans, while she was defended by Mr. Wharton, whose defence revolved around claiming the woman on the bridge was not Hall. She was found guilty and sentenced to 3 months hard labour.

32.
THE STAIR CASE
7 Oct 1892

At 32 Savoy Street on September 17th, Catherine Dunbannon went to bed, leaving her husband downstairs. She was sober, and he was drunk. Later he shouted "Come downstairs you ***." She did not answer, so he went upstairs. Their lodger Eliza Ann Walker heard the sound of a body being dragged across the floor to the top of the stairs.

Mr. Dunbannon said "Take that, you ***", and knocked her down the stairs. He said "Get up, Kate", and dragged her into the front room. Walker went downstairs the next day and found Mrs. Dunbannon lying in a corner of the room on a bed and mattress due to be thrown out. Walker asked how she felt; she said "Oh, my head and back is bad". On October 4th, surgeon HE Hackett of Gorton was called for, and saw her during a bad epileptic seizure. He was told she had been in fits for two days. He said there was nothing to suggest violence. She was moved to Withington Workhouse Hospital.

JS Orchard, resident house surgeon at the Hospital, saw her on October 5th; she was practically constantly fitting. When she died on October 7th, he wrote the death certificate, giving naturally-occurring convulsions as the cause of death. Walker neglected to bring up the incident to the doctors, and did not mention it to anyone until October 30th, when Dunbannon was treating her and her children badly. Her son said "If you've killed your wife, you are not going to kill my mother." He thrashed the lad, causing Walker to send for a policeman. Neighbours also knew Dunbannon had thrown his wife down the stairs.

Shortly after the funeral at Philips Park Cemetery, he and some friends quarrelled, and it was revealed that she was murdered. The body was exhumed on November 3rd.

Sidney Smelt, deputy City coroner, held an inquest on November 4th at the City Coroner's Court. Margaret Price, her sister, said she had not seen her sister for some years before seeing her dead at Withington Hospital. A woman she did not know told her Mr. Dunbannon had thrown her down the stairs; she was hesitant to inform police, because she did not know if this was true. WJ Heslop, police surgeon, conducted a post-mortem examination. He found congestion of the brain, usual with epilepsy sufferers, but nothing to suggest the fall had anything to do with her death. If the fall really had caused her death, there would be greater brain trauma.
The jury returned a verdict in accordance with the medical evidence. Dunbannon was called back in, and Smelt asked him why he did not report the fall to the doctors.

"She fell downstairs. She was not hurt by the fall at all, and she was out drinking with Mrs. Walker on the Sunday that she fell on the Saturday". Walker denied this. Dunbannon said "I did not pitch her downstairs". "I think you did, and I think you are very lucky that you did not kill her".

33.
TEMPER LOST IN GORTON
29 Oct 1892

Samuel Meadowcroft (32) was an engine tenter at a warehouse close to the police court in Manchester. He lived with his wife Margaret Ann (35), who he had married in 1880, at 18 Thomas Street, Gorton.
At 6:20pm on a Saturday evening, October 29th, they went up to PC Albert Moore, who was on duty on Gorton Lane. Meadowcroft told him there was a rough lot on Thomas Street, and if he saw any bother to stand at the top of Thomas Street and watch it. A little later that evening Joseph Brown, a clothes dealer, bought some clothes from the Meadowcrofts.

At 10:15pm they visited a pawnbroker, TW Mitchell (Gorton Lane), and made a purchase. Both men saw them on friendly terms. Meadowcroft drunkenly turned himself in at the Town Hall's detective office on October 30th at 4:00pm, and gave a statement to Chief Detective Inspector Caminada. Caminada and police surgeon WJ Heslop, accompanied by Sgt. Nelson, went to his house.

They found Margaret on the floor with her head battered in, blood spattered all over the kitchen floor, wallpaper and wainscoting. Her teeth had been loosened and her face disfigured. The body was taken to the Fairfield Street station mortuary, where Heslop performed a post-mortem examination.
She had 11 broken ribs and two severe bruises on her throat, 15 on her chest, one on her left collarbone, on the back of her left hand and on her right arm. She had bruises on the external corners of both eyes, a badly contused abdomen and marks on her legs indicative of violence. The breast bone was broken across at the junction of the upper third and middle third. The 1st, 5th, 6th, 7th and 8th ribs on the

right were fractured. On the left, the 6th, 7th, 8th, 9th, 10th and 11th ribs were fractured. The liver was ruptured and torn right through. The cause of death was given as shock and haemorrhage from the rupture of the liver, but there were apparently sufficient injuries without that to cause death. The injuries were so severe that Heslop believed Meadowcroft had jumped on his wife.
Later that evening Caminada charged him with murdering his wife, and he was taken into custody.

He appeared at the City Police Court on October 31st, before RR Armitage, R Hall and Alderman Lloyd. He confessed, but denied having used any weapons. Caminada produced a written statement DI Hargreaves had written, on account of how "extraordinary" his admission was. It read *"I, Samuel Meadowcroft, of 18, Thomas-street, West Gorton, say:- I went to the house at half-past 11 last night (Saturday). Some one else was in the house. I could hear them talking. I tried the door. It was fast, and when it was opened I was met with a poker. I wanted to know who had been in the house, but I could get no satisfaction. I went the back way. The yard door was open and the scullery door was open. My wife struck at me again with the poker. I took the poker from her and hit her with my fist. I found her in the same place at about 5:30 this morning. I carried her upstairs, and left her on the room floor, and threw her skirts over her, where she is now. I make this statement of my own free will, and I have been cautioned by Chief Detective Inspector Caminada."* He told the magistrates that Meadowcroft and his wife led a miserable life with their young son, (despite apparently being on good terms the night of the murder when they both went out shopping). Caminada successfully applied for a remand until November 1st after the coroner's inquest.

The inquest was held on November 4th by deputy City coroner Sidney Smelt. Solicitor TE Gibbons represented Meadowcroft. Her father Michael Wynne (30 Tipping Street, Ardwick) identified the body. He said their relationship was unhappy to drink, which Samuel had forced her into: to this accusation Gibbons said "Oh that will not do". Wynne went on to say that they had lived together except for a period of nearly 3 years, when he left home about a year after their wedding.

Aaron Travis, their next-door neighbour, said he saw Mrs. Meadowcroft walk past his house alone, and clearly very drunk, just after 11:00pm on the night of the murder. Samuel followed shortly after and walked straight into his house. Just after midnight he heard two slight screams. He had heard them quarrel four or five times over the course of 10 or 12 weeks he had been living next to them.

Isabella Willingham, another next-door neighbour, said she had heard two screams between 11:00pm and 11:30pm that night. She also told the court that on the last two Saturdays before the murder she had heard Samuel beating her while they were both drunk. She had told Margaret to knock on the wall when he was hitting her. She said she had never known Margaret to have male guests.

A woman named Gresty attested to Meadowcroft's violence, saying he had hit Margaret on October 15th.
Sarah Ann Barlow, a neighbour, said she had met Margaret at Gorton Brook that night, and had both gone to the Pineapple Hotel on Pottery Lane. They returned to Thomas Street at 11:10pm. She said goodnight to Margaret, who she claimed was not sober at the time, and left.
William Mundy, landlord of the Pineapple, said Samuel had been in the pub that night. He said Barlow and Margaret both left just before 11:00pm when he stopped serving them as they were very drunk.

Gibbons said Samuel was a hard-working man, and his wife often pawned his things without permission.
He appeared before the City Police Court on November 2nd. He *"wore that dejected air which characterised his appearance at the inquest"*,

and again sat with his head in his hands and his arms on his knees. He was committed to the assizes for trial.

He appeared at the Manchester Assizes on December 1st, and was sentenced to 10 years' penal servitude for manslaughter.

34.
THE BROTHERS OF PICCADILLY
28 Nov 1892

John Meyrick (Stanley Grove, Longsight) and John Swindells (21, a labourer of 27 Glebe Street, Longsight) killed Meyrick's brother William (21, a gas stoker of 91 Lever Street) on the corner of Dale and Lever Streets, Piccadilly on a Monday at about 7:00pm. They had been quarreling on the corner of Lever Street and Stevenson Square, because Meyrick had hit William's fellow-lodger earlier that evening. It appears Swindells and William were both angry at Meyrick. William hit Meyrick, and Meyrick hit him back, but apparently not in the face. Meyrick said to William, "Shake hands; shake hands, Bill," and offered his hand. William said "I would not shake hands with a man like you".

Alexander Farquhar (91 Lever Street) came up and told William to come home. William said "Alright, I will go in a minute", then punched his brother in the face or chest, calling him "a hard-hearted ***". Meyrick punched him twice in retaliation. Farquhar pulled William away, but he got loose and chased the others. He punched Swindells, who staggered back, then punched him in the face. He staggered backwards and Farquhar caught him. Farquhar told Swindells and Meyrick to leave, and they crossed the square. He pulled William away, but got less than 30 yards away before William said "No, I'll have them yet", and chased them down Lever Street. He talked to his brother, and Swindells began to interfere.

He pushed Swindells, who staggered backwards, then punched William two or three times hard in the face. He fell against the wall and then slumped onto the floor. William Sorah, a cabman, pulled Swindells away and threatened to give him in to the police if he touched William again. Swindells left the scene, leaving Farquhar and Meyrick tending to William.

All of them had been drinking, with William particularly worse for wear. At 7:00pm PC Jonas Mason arrived, and saw William lying on the ground, apparently fitting. The crowd accused Meyrick and Swindells, and he arrested them. William was taken on a litter to the Infirmary, where JW Smith, resident surgical officer, told Mason he had died. Meyrick said "He hit me, and I struck him back again". Swindells was arrested at 11:15pm for causing the death, and said "What I did was in self-defence". They were brought before TC Horsfall at the City Police Court on November 29th, and remanded until December 2nd.

Sidney Smelt, deputy City coroner, held an inquest on November 30th at the City Coroner's Court. Francis Meyrick, their father, had to come from Oswestry to identify the body. JW Smith, who conducted the post-mortem examination, said there was a circular bruise on the right temple, with extravasation underneath. The cause of death was given as pressure on the brain from this extravasation of blood. The inquest was adjourned to December 2nd to allow Swindells and Meyrick to give evidence.
On December 2nd, Meyrick and Swindells gave corroborative evidence that obviously incriminated Swindells. The coroner brought up that Swindells had once killed a man in a prize fight, and was tried for manslaughter but acquitted. He asked that this not influence the jury, as the point of the inquest was to ascertain whether the aggression Swindells used on November 28th was really in self-defence. A verdict of manslaughter was returned after some deliberation. He was committed for trial at the Liverpool Assizes on the coroner's warrant. Meyrick was discharged. Swindell was discharged at the Assizes on December 15th due to a lack of evidence, and the likelihood that William "brought it upon himself".

35.
THE DRUNKARD AND THE LAMP
18 Dec 1892

Robert Tomlinson, an umbrella maker, lived with his wife Ann on Cheltenham Street, Collyhurst. According to Ann, he came home drunk on a Saturday night, December 17th, and asked for beer. She did not give him any, and he went to sleep. She went out, and when she got back he asked for more beer. She brought him a pint, and he asked for more later, but it was past closing time. He threatened to assault her, and they went to bed together. When they got upstairs he pushed her over and kicked her in the eye, knocking her into the corner.

His son Matthew (4) and daughter began to cry. He got into bed, and as she was leaning over Matthew, who slept at the foot of their bed, he tried to kick her, and knocked the lamp she was holding onto the child. The lamp exploded and set Matthew, his clothes and bed on fire, killing him almost immediately. He was given to their neighbour, Mrs. Allen, who took him to Dr. Taylor (Rochdale Road) just before 12:00am that night. He died the next day on December 18th. He appeared at the City Police Court on December 19th, and was remanded until December 23rd.

An inquest was held the same day at the City Coroner's Court by deputy City coroner Sidney Smelt. Tomlinson claimed he had been in bed 15 minutes before his wife came up. As soon as she did, she picked up the lamp, removed the chimney and threw the lamp onto the bed. He threw their daughter into a corner of the room to protect her, but it burnt Matthew. He smothered Matthew in a blanket and gave him to Mrs. Allen.

Mrs. Allen was called upon, and said she had heard the Tomlinsons quarrel that night, and had gone in to see Matthew badly burnt. Mrs. Tomlinson told her it was Robert's fault, and he denied it, saying she had thrown the lamp at him. The coroner said the case could not be further investigated and there was no evidence to support either account. The jury returned a verdict of 'death from burns'. The coroner said he was highly suspicious of Robert, on account of him being a drunk and of bad character. He hoped the death of the child would be punishment enough if he really had caused it. On the morning of December 31st, he was sentenced to 1 month of hard labour for assaulting his wife at the City Police Court.

36.
THE HAMMER AT REDDISH
19 Jun 1893

Thomas Baxendale (56), a practically-retired spinner, lived in a 4-room terraced cottage on Newton Street, Reddish, with his wife Ann (55) and 4 of their 5 sons, all of whom were employed at the mill of the Reddish Spinning Co. Ltd.. He slept in the front bedroom with his wife and the two younger sons (17 and 15). His second-eldest son was about to be married, and was going to buy a house in the next street. They were from Bolton, and had lived in Reddish about 20 years, since the mill was set up. His eldest son was married to the daughter of the mill's manager. They were hard-working and saved up their wages. He saved £200 that he invested back into the company.

Money was kept in their bank account connected to the mill, for which there was a 5% interest. In about 1883 he emigrated to work for Messrs. Coates & Co., New Jersey, leaving her behind. Before he left Liverpool he transferred the £200 to her. In New Jersey he made a lot of money, and sent some of it occasionally to his wife to add to her little "pile". He returned home in early 1887, and asked her to return the money to him. She and her sons objected.

On March 10th, 1887, he cut his throat, and was admitted to Stockport Infirmary. He was discharged a fortnight later and brought before the city magistrates at Strangeways. He was discharged on the condition that he be properly cared for by his family. Since then they quarrelled about the money more and more often, but it was never particularly violent.

He was not known to drink, but did indulge in "sprees" (binge-drinking). He was well-known by his neighbours as being scrupulously honest and never being indebted. Recently he was considered a little slow, the *Manchester Courier* commented that "*people now shake their heads and say, "I thought he was little bit off it"*". In 1892 or 1893 his wife took out a summons against him for assault, but the matter was settled before going to court, and they went on holiday to the Isle of Man. There, he bought a pocket knife.

On Sunday, June 18th, 1893, he asked his wife for a shilling. She did not give it him, and he went to bed sober. At 2:00am on a Monday morning, he was heard having words with her. At 3:00am he got up and walked about the house. He told his son Albert Edward Ernest that he would drink all the brandy in the house to see if it would send him to sleep or make him crazy. At 5:30am the sons went to work, leaving Baxendale dressed, sitting downstairs, reading the newspaper as usual.

At 6:05am neighbours heard "Murder!", and a neighbour, Daniel Thompson Heyworth, looked through the back window and saw Baxendale and his wife lying on the floor. He sent a boy to the mill for the sons, and a messenger for the police. PC Irvine went to the house and broke in, finding Mrs. Baxendale lying dead in a pool of blood at the foot of the staircase in the back kitchen. Under her clothing was a heavy coal hammer, with a shaft a foot long. Her head and face were badly wounded. There was a 5"-long, deep wound on the left side of the throat that had slashed her windpipe and jugular vein. Her fingers had been cut through trying to defend herself.

Her cheek was cut, and there was an indented wound on her forehead. Her husband was lying next to her with his throat cut, faint from the blood loss. Irvine asked him what had happened, and he said "I have done it, let me die too. I have been driven to it", and admitted "I did it with my pocket knife", which was in his trousers pocket, wiped clean. He said "I struck my wife on the head with a hammer, and then cut her throat. I cut my own throat, but becoming unnerved did not make a proper job of it".

Dr. Smith was sent for; he bandaged Baxendale's wounds and sent him to Stockport Infirmary under the care of Sgt. Scarth. His wounds were not particularly bad, so recovery was expected. It transpired he had attempted suicide before, and had often threatened his wife violently.

An inquest was held in Reddish on June 21st by Mr. Price, returning a verdict of wilful murder against Baxendale. By June 23rd it was hoped that he would improve enough to send him before the magistrates soon. The case was tried at the Manchester City Police Court on July 11th; Sgt. Bent gave the details of the case. Baxendale had told his friends he wanted nobody to defend him or speak on his behalf in court.

He was remanded for a week. He was received into custody on July 18th. The grand jury of Liverpool Assizes' Crown Court returned a true bill on July 28th. Mr. Mulholland successfully applied for the case to be tried at the same court on July 31st. The defence stated that Baxendale was under the influence of *delirium tremens*, brought on "by his own evil habits of life". The judge, John Compton Lawrence, practically stopped the case at this point, and the jury returned a verdict that he was of unsound mind when he committed the murder. He was sentenced to life in an asylum.

37.
THE BABE IN THE WOODS
30 Jul 1893

Elizabeth Ann Remington was a domestic servant for Ashworth Reed, a manufacturer at Spruce Mill, Burnley. She was also the mother of his illegitimate son, born in June. At the beginning of July she went, on his orders, to Manchester from Burnley Station, and lodged on New Bridge Street. She had lodged there for 3 months already, but from July onwards she stayed confined to the house. Reed sent her money to support her. She wrote to him "I should like to see you on Sunday if you can make it convenient. Signed your affectionate friend, Elizabeth Allen".

On Sunday, July 30th she met him at Victoria Station, telling her housekeeper she was going to meet her uncle to go to her stepmother's house in Kirby Lonsdale. She gave, or had given, the landlady a ring that she claimed Reed had given her. They walked up to Ducie Bridge and took a tram to Cheetham Hill. They walked to Boggart Hole Clough, a wooded area in Blackley. He soaked a handkerchief in water and gave it to her to put over her son's mouth. She did it, and took it off again. Then he did it. Believing his son to be dead, he wrapped him in clothes and put him in a brown parcel, tied it and left it in the woods. He returned to Burnley, leaving her on New Bridge Street.

She wrote to him, and he replied telling her nobody would ever trace the murder back to her. He said he could never hold his head up again in Burnley if word got out that he had fathered an illegitimate child. He told her to write to him under the name of "Richard Battersby" at Spruce Mill.

The parcel was found on August 6th by PC Butler. On September 21st the Chief Constable opened the case into the death, and went with Inspector Goodwin to New Bridge Street. They showed her the clothes; she said she had lent them to Remington to wrap the child in that day. She directed them to Burnley, and from there found Remington's address and arrested her on September 28th.

She implicated Reed, who was then arrested at the Royal Exchange on the morning of September 29th by Chief Detective Inspector Caminada. He took Reed to the Detective's Office and got a statement from Remington. He read Reed this statement; he replied "it will be better for me to say nothing now". WJ Heslop, police surgeon, had his assistant conduct the post-mortem examination and found the death to be from convulsions.

The case was tried at the Manchester City Police Court before R. Hall and other magistrates on the afternoon of September 29th. Caminada wanted Heslop to tell the inquest that the death was similar to one from suffocation. Mr. Beckton (of Hockin, Raby & Beckton) appeared for Reed. Beckton objected on the grounds that Heslop was giving expert opinion rather than an informed analysis, because he had not actually performed the examination.

Nevertheless Heslop agreed with Caminada. They were remanded until October 6th, bail being refused. He was acquitted by the Liverpool Assizes on November 23rd, and appeared at the Manchester Royal Exchange on November 24th, where he was protested against so aggressively that he had to hide in the office of the Master of the Exchange. He was smuggled out of the building, but was chased for 100 yards before he was finally left alone.

38.
NEGLECT ON POTT STREET
8 Jul 1893

Mary Mellor, 2 years old, died in a children's shelter in Ancoats on a Saturday. She had lived with her mother Ann at 15 Pott Street, Ancoats, where they had moved in April. Ann was a rag picker who earned only 8s. a week at the most, and usually put Mary in the care of some women in the neighbourhood, whom she paid 1s. 6d. or 2s. a week. On Pott Street she was looked after by Mrs. Eliza Duke, whom she promised to pay 2s. a week, but Mellor had to buy the food; during the time the child had been with Duke, she had only brought food 2 or 3 times.

Eventually Mary became very ill and emaciated from lack of nourishment. On July 1st Duke told Mellor to take her to a doctor; she refused, and Duke said she would have nothing more to do with the child. Duke checked on them on July 5th and found Mary lying unconscious on the floor in a filthy room. She took Mary to the police station, and a doctor told her Mary was 13¼lbs. underweight at just 11¾lbs. when clothed.

On the afternoon of July 7th she was taken to the Cannel Street station; PC Buchanan went for Mellor, and took her into custody. Mary was examined by WJ Heslop, police surgeon. She was covered in flea bites, and drank ravenously when offered milk and water. She was then taken to the children's shelter where she died. Heslop performed the post-mortem examination, and found that she had tuberculosis, enlarged mesenteric glands and an entire absence of fat.

She appeared at the City Police Court on July 8th; Mary was in the care of the Manchester and Salford Society for the Prevention of Cruelty to Children. John Ashley, a Society inspector, said she was too ill to be taken to court. It was not expected that she would live. Mellor was remanded for a week. When Ashley got back to the Society shelter that day he found Mary had died. Heslop attributed the death to tuberculosis, accelerated and exacerbated by her mother's neglect. He believed the death was easily avoided by proper medical attention. Mellor was arrested by a constable; she told him she had neglected the child since she took it out of hospital. When she was charged with causing its death, she said "How could I cause the death of the child when I was out at work?"

She appeared before Mr. Justice Kennedy at the Manchester Crown Court on July 14th. Mr. Parry prosecuted, and Mr. Crompton Smith defended. Smith's defence revolved around the fact Mellor was poor and literally could not support her child. The judge said it was still Mellor's duty to get her child attended to, and by criminally neglecting to do so had caused the death, whether directly or indirectly. Mr. Parry argued that in Manchester a child could easily be attended to, whether in hospital or by a private doctor. A verdict of not guilty was returned, and she was acquitted.

39.
NEGLECT ON PETER STREET
27 Oct 1893

Elsie Hibbert was the illegitimate child of Mary Hibbert (40), who lodged at 13 Peter Street, Openshaw, away from her husband, a boiler maker at sea. She was born on December 19th, 1892. Mr. Hibbert had left his wife in 1891, but returned from sea in August 1893 in a cab. His wife ran for Mrs. Annie Cooke, and begged her husband not to hurt her. He lived with her a few days and then sold the house off and kicked her out.

Elsie and Mary then went to stay with a Mrs. Watson for a day, before trying to live with her mother, hoping she would forgive her "misfortune". Elsie stayed with Watson while her mother went to live with her grandmother for five days. When Hibbert got back she found lodgings at 13 Peter Street, with a charwoman, Sarah Schofield (46). Schofield was herself a lodger under Mrs. Evans, tenant. Hibbert would leave Elsie in Schofield's care for 4s. a week while she went to work at the Blue Shed, Openshaw as a weaver for 16s. a week.

She would then take care of Elsie at night, and came home in her lunch hour to check on her. Elsie had been taken to Withington Workhouse with diarrhoea on August 9th. She apparently had 4 other children in there that she did not deal with, and another 2 lived with her mother in Staines.

She discharged Elsie on August 14th. On August 16th she took her to the Clinical Hospital to get some medicine. Elsie did not improve, and Dr. HE Hackett, of Gorton, was consulted in September. He said she was suffering mildly from a wasting ailment, probably due to improper feeding. He visited them four times, and each time was satisfied that the baby was being cared for. On his advice she took a fortnight of work to care for Elsie. He did not believe anything Hibbert had done or not done had caused the illness.

On the 4th visit he told her to visit Dr. Jones, because Hackett was not in her district. Jones saw Elsie on September 13th, and thought her condition could be recovered from.

On the second visit Elsie was brought in by Schofield's little daughter; another child brought her on the third visit, but he sent her back and told her to bring Hibbert. Hibbert told Schofield on October 10th that she was not looking after Elsie well enough; Schofield told her to "take her bastard child away". Jones brought her condition to the attention of John Ashley, an inspector of On October 13th, Elizabeth Hindley (7 Halston Street, Openshaw) said she Elsie blue with cold in her cradle at 13 Peter Street on the morning of October 13th. She was alone, Schofield having gone out charring.

Jones was "thunderstruck" when he saw Elsie on October 16th; she was a "living skeleton", and he never expected her to recover. He informed the Manchester & Salford Society for the Prevention of Cruelty to Children. John Ashley, a Society inspector, visited the home the same day. He immediately took Elsie to the Society shelter on Chatham Street, Piccadilly, and then to Dr. Young (5 Stockport Road, Ardwick) the same day. She weighed 10lb 7oz. (9lb lighter than the average weight). She was jaundiced, skeletal, with a practically non-existent pulse and a concave abdomen with very thin walls.

The slightest pressure on her abdominal wall would touch her backbone. Her leg muscles were rigid due to lying in one position for so long, and there was a bed sore on her thigh. Her eyes rolled listlessly until she was offered milk, which she drank quickly. He believed her condition was due to starvation. Photographs of the house and baby were taken. Schofield and Hibbert were brought by the Society to the City Police Court on October 27th, prosecuted by Mr. Overend Evans.

The case was adjourned for a week because it was believed the baby would soon be dead, and the Coroner hoped to bring the women up on a manslaughter charge. Witnesses attested to Hibbert's industrious nature, but Ashley said both women were drunk when he visited the house. Schofield was granted bail, but never paid it. Elsie died later that day.

An inquest was held by Sidney Smelt, deputy City coroner, at the City Coroner's Court on November 1st. Hibbert said she had always given Elsie plenty of milk, but she could not keep it down. She said she had taken a 2-week hiatus from work to tend to Elsie, and tried to find new lodgings, unsuccessfully.

Annie Cooke (probably a Society officer) gave a statement that she had seen Elsie when she was born, and called her a beautiful baby. When Elsie left the workhouse, she looked gravely ill. She visited the house many times. On the first visit, Hibbert asked if she could procure some milk for Elsie, because she had none left. She told Cooke she only had one meal for herself that week, being out of work, but would go without if it meant Elsie had food. Cooke called at the house around September 21st and saw Elsie nude; Schofield said she had had to strip her because she and her clothes were filthy.

The room, including her cradle, were also in a terrible state. When Hibbert got home, Cooke asked her if she had been giving Elsie her medicine; she said "No, what's the use in giving it medicine?" While she was there, neither Hibbert nor Schofield attended to Elsie in any way.

She saw Elsie a week later, lying undressed on the floor. She gave her a cup of milk, and she grabbed it, and drank it ravenously. She told the women they were not caring properly for the baby, and Hibbert said "I feed it when I come home from work, and look after it as well as I can. No-one will have me, except Mrs. Schofield." At this, Schofield said "I wish you had never come here". The next Wednesday Cooke visited again, and did not even take Elsie out of her cradle because she looked so ill. When Hibbert got home, Cooke told her she would not be visiting again unless they moved to a cleaner home.

Mrs. Hindley said Schofield got drunk a lot and was often seen out of the house, leaving Elsie alone. Mrs. Evans said she had once offered to feed Elsie, but Schofield said "Mind your own business". This was supported by neighbours Margaret Hibbert and Mary Wroe. Mrs. Taylor, matron of the shelter, said Elsie was practically a skeleton when she was admitted.

Paediatrician Dr. Ashby, of the Manchester Children's Hospital, conducted the post-mortem; he found her death to be due to exhaustion from starvation, which she suffered on account of the badly deteriorated state of her stomach and bowels from severe diarrhoea. He agreed it was a case of neglect; had Elsie been fed properly at night, she would not be so ill. A juror asked why Schofield was not present; she was in prison, having failed to pay bail. The jury asked to hear from Hackett, Young and the workhouse doctor Grohard, so the inquest was adjourned until November 2nd. The requested witnesses, and two nurses (one being Annie Williams) attended.

Grohard said Elsie had not suffered diarrhoea while in hospital, but a small skin eruption. He said other than this, Elsie was quite healthy; Williams attested to this, saying she was a "remarkably fine" child. The other nurse said she was as heavy as a baby four months older than her. At this, Hibbert claimed that when Elsie was discharged she was in such a bad state she could hardly recognise her.

Schofield never attended court on account of being in prison, and Smelt did not believe her statement was beneficial to the jury. The jury returned a verdict of manslaughter against Hibbert and Schofield, and its foreman complimented Ashley for his work, and the Coroner praised the Society.

They were tried at the Manchester Winter Assizes Crown Court on February 23rd, 1894, before Mr. Justice Arthur Charles. Mr Parry prosecuted, and Schofield and Hibbert were undefended. A witness said Hibbert was hard-working and left for work at 6:00am every day. They were found guilty and sentenced to 130 days hard labour each. Later that day the judge brought them back, and told them that since they had been in prison for quite a while already, the sentence would be from January 1st.

40.
THE CLEGG STREET BABY
9 Dec 1893

Ellen McMonagle (30), lodging on Clegg Street, Rochdale Road, killed her newborn illegitimate daughter. She had left her cousin's house on nearby Hannah Street on December 5th after being replaced by another lodger. While on Hannah Street she had started to look and complain of being ill. McMonagle had been a domestic servant for a justice of the peace for seven years.

On December 8th she found lodgings on Clegg Street with a Miss Farrell, who accepted her on the condition she go back to Hannah Street the next day. On December 9th she did not get up all day, and complained of having a very bad night. At 9:00pm Farrell heard a noise as if someone had fallen; she went upstairs and found McMonagle on her hands and knees on the bedroom floor with specks of blood about her.

Farrell offered to fetch a doctor, but she refused. She left McMonagle with a neighbour, who later told Farrell she thought she had given birth. McMonagle denied this, saying she had been suffering from dropsy. She later confessed; the bed was searched, and a baby was found dead, compressed between the mattresses. Her face was injured. She was arrested, and taken to Crumpsall Hospital some days later. She was too ill to appear at the inquest by Deputy Coroner Sidney Smelt.

She left the hospital on the morning of January 8th, 1894, and was arrested by DS Harris at the Town Hall. She said she would say nothing about it until she saw her solicitor. Later that day she was brought before Francis John Headlam, the stipendiary magistrate at the City Police Court, and was found guilty of wilful murder and concealment. Harris successfully applied for a remand until December 10th, on account of her being very weak. She appeared before the City Police Court on January 16th. The testament of Dr. Ashby, who conducted the post-mortem, was heard.

He said the death was caused by skull injuries, but he could not say how. She was committed for trial at the Assizes at 10:00am on February 23rd on a charge of murder. The judge, Mr. Justice Charles, said the sentence could be one for wilful murder, manslaughter, or concealment of birth. For concealment, she was sentenced to 8 months' hard labour.

41.
THE BRADFORD BUS
25 Dec 1893

5-year-old Joseph Nicholas O'Neill, a lithographic printer's son of Burns Street, Bradford, was walking down nearby Mill Street with his elder brother after dinner to play. They were joined by another boy, Sherratt. They were going out to play. They were going to cross Wilson Street, off Mill Street; O'Neill got three yards across, and the others were just about to step off the pavement when Sherratt saw a three-horse bus gallop round the corner into Wilson Street.

He shouted, but the bus was only four yards away from O'Neil; it knocked him down and killed him. The driver, Edmund Jones did not stop, and went on to the stables. After the incident he was found by police sergeant Preston Hartley, who believed he was drunk.

An inquest was held on December 27th by Sidney Smelt, deputy City coroner, at the City Coroner's Court. Lots of evidence was heard, some contradictory. The jury found Jones guilty of gross negligence and returned a verdict of manslaughter. He was committed on the coroner's warrant to the Assizes.

He was brought before the magistrates at the City Police Court on December 28th. His defence was that the 3 horses in his charge were only walking at the time; prosecution stated he had been given plenty of warning before he hit O'Neill. He was committed to the Assizes for trial on a charge of manslaughter. O'Neill was buried on December 30th in a public grave in Philips Park Cemetery.

Jones appeared at the Assizes on February 22nd, defended by Mr. Jordan; Mr. Acton prosecuted. Jordan maintained it was an accident, and Jones had been working well as a driver for two decades. The jury returned a verdict of not guilty, and he was acquitted.

42.
'SOMETHING TO DO' IN CHORLTON
3 Mar 1894

Cattle drover Richard Hodgins killed charwoman Miss Susannah "Annie" Dobson (39) at their home at 3 Fairfield Street, Chorlton-on-Medlock, at about 8:00pm on a Saturday night. They had had a fight, and went to sleep on the sofa. When he woke up at 4:00am the next morning he had his arm around her waist, cuddling her. He apparently had no idea what had happened. He shouted "Annie", or said "Get me a drink of water, Annie", and after hearing no response and feeling her cold skin, lit a light and found her dead.

Hodgins got to his sister Martha Farrand's house (3 Mount Place) at 5:00am, and was heard by neighbour Elizabeth Washington knocking on her door. She refused to open the door, and he shouted that when she knew what had happened, she would open the door. Washington went downstairs and talked to him, and he asked for some water. He was badly trembling, and when she asked what was wrong he said "Oh, there's something to do". Farrand came in, and Hodgins told her Dobson was dead.

She said she did not believe him; he said "Yes, she's dead enough". He told her what he knew, then took two purses from his pocket and gave Farrand the contents. Farrand said she was going to tell the police; he said he wished he had some poison so he could kill himself.

Farrand and Washington said they would go and see Dobson to check if Hodgins was telling the truth, and the three of them walked to the corner of Brook Street. He left them, saying he would go and kill himself. Farrand told him to go to see their brother in Ancoats. He walked away, but came running back to them when they got to Cook Street, saying he had found the key to his house. They walked to Fairfield Street, where Hodgins struck a light and they all saw Dobson's body. He said it was an awful thing, and claimed he had no idea what had happened.

When they left, he went up Cook Street towards his brother John's house (Pollard Street, Ancoats), and the women went to the police station on Cavendish Street. Two constables, Fawcett and Patrick Lacey, went to the house and found it in a state of disarray, with furniture upside down and a chair broken on the floor. The sofa and the area around it had blood on them, and a rolling pin, poker and chair leg near the sofa also had blood marks on them. She was badly wounded and bruised, with a bad gash on her forehead or temple which had split her skull. In the backyard there was a broken broom handle covered in blood, and a bucket containing bloody water. He then went to arrest Hodgins.

Hodgins arrived at John's house at about 6:00am, saying "I have done it, I have killed Annie". He sat down and cried. John asked how it happened; Hodgins said "She hit me with a chair, and I hit her with a chair leg". Just then, Lacey and Fawcett came in and arrested him. He said "I have nothing to say"; his clothes were covered in blood. He tried to give a statement to Fawcett, who warned him to keep cool and be careful about what he was going to say. Hodgins said he thought the murder might have happened between 11:00pm and 12:00pm on March 3rd, but he was unsure. He was equally unsure about whether it was done with a chair leg. He said he was going to turn himself in when they arrived.

Sidney Smelt, deputy City coroner, opened the inquest on March 5th at the City Coroner's Court. He appeared, guarded by 2 policemen. He was shabbily-dressed and "somewhat dissipated in appearance". Dobson was identified by her sister, Mrs. Isabella Smith (107 Trafford Road, Salford), who had seen Dobson 3 weeks ago in good health, and did not know she was living with Hodgins.

Ann Lynch (1 Fairfield Street) said Dobson was in her house on March 3rd; at 5:00pm Lynch put Dobson to sleep on the sofa, because she was badly drunk. She said she heard no disturbance from Hodgins' house all night, despite her going to bed early on March 4th. She did say, however, that she was a heavy sleeper, and admitted having had "a drink or two" that night. She said she had often had to intervene when Hodgins and Dobson fought.

To this, Hodgins asked if she was aware that Dobson sometimes threw things at him. She said she was aware, and was also aware that Hodgins and Dobson had spent 5 hours on March 3rd out shopping and drinking. Thomas Leary (5 Fairfield Street) said he had heard Dobson scream several times between 5:00pm and 6:00pm on the evening of March 3rd.
The Coroner asked Hodgins if he wanted Farrand called in; he agreed, and Farrand gave a statement that corroborated Washington's account.

In response to Lacey's account, Hodgins stated the rolling pin was in a drawer, and the hammer was in the coal hole. Police surgeon WJ Heslop said he had visited the house, and found Dobson with her hands and arms smeared with blood, an ugly gash on her forehead, her upper lip split and a punctured wound just under the left corner of the mouth. There was a large bloodstain on the hearthstone, another on the right upright of the mantelpiece and a third on the floor near the sofa. A post-mortem found that there was an inch-long scar behind the left ear extending to the bone, and six punctured wounds behind it.

There were four bad bruises on the front of the chest and various others on her arms, sides and legs. They corresponded with a blunt object like the chair leg. He found human hair and blood on the hammer, but believed this was because she had fallen on it. Her windpipe was badly bruised. The cause of death was given as syncope from haemorrhage and shock. Hodgins said he was very sorry but declined to give a statement. A verdict of wilful murder was returned, and he was committed to trial on the coroner's warrant. He was brought before Francis John Headlam (stipendiary magistrate) at the City Police Court that afternoon, and committed to the Liverpool Assizes.

He appeared before Mr. Justice Day on March 15th, and was sentenced to death. JF Leese, Q.C. and MP for Accrington, prosecuted; he said that if there was ever a case caused by drink, it was this one.

3 friends visited him in Walton Gaol, Liverpool on March 27th, and saw him in the interview room. He looked well, but "gave vent to impassioned cries for liberty". He became calmer towards the end of the interview and gave them a sincere and affectionate goodbye. He praised the treatment he had received by the warders and governor, and commented that he had not been left alone during his time there.

Farrand visited him on the afternoon of March 29th. He was not bearing up well, and professed his innocence vehemently. She told him a reprieve petition had been presented by MP HJ Cust, and started by the Home Secretary; he expressed gratitude, and said that in his heart he knew he did not deserve to hang. He said he had no malice towards Dobson, but wished he had taken his friends' advice and left her a long time ago. Farrand said he was "one of the best fellows going" when sober, and was a model son and good lad to their mother.

On March 31st, the governor of Walton Gaol received a telegraph from the Home Office ordering a reprieve. He respited the sentence to penal servitude for life on April 6th, and Hodgins he was freed from Portland Prison on March 6th, 1914.

43.
THE SMASHED WINDOW

18 Sep 1894

Ann Hollingworth and her husband George quarrelled at their home of 17 Napier Street, Miles Platting on a Monday night. Neighbours heard a window smashing. She was found by a neighbour lying at the top of the stairs at her home, just before 10:00am the next morning. She had died from a cut to her wrist.

Her husband was at work, and was arrested later and taken to the station on Cannel Street, where his wife's body was being kept. An inquest was held on September 19th; the jury returned a verdict of 'accidental death' after Hollingworth confessed to quarreling with his wife, and said Ann had cut her wrist by smashing the window.

44.
THE ANCOATS BOATMEN
19 Nov 1894

Ann Jane Mooney (24), a labourer's new wife, woke up early on a dark and foggy Monday morning at her home of 5 Tuke Street, Ancoats. Her husband Patrick woke at 6:30am and believed she was making breakfast, as usual, and went back to sleep. Just before 7:00am she threw herself, and her 5-month-old son John into the Rochdale Canal off Union Street, Ancoats. A boathouse keeper, Thomas Seddon (3 Berry's Buildings, Salford) heard her shout and the splash of her hitting the water.

He ran along the towpath and saw her struggling in the water. He and other men were bringing barges under the bridge, and threw her a boat-hook. He jumped onto a passing boat, got a shaft and held it out. She grabbed it and he hoisted her onto the boat. She said "My baby is gone!". Seddon asked where he was, and she lifted him from the water by his leg. Another man, Alps or Helps, came onto the boat and leant over the side of the boat to take the baby. It was clear he was dying. Mooney shouted "Save me, master, save me", and they hoisted her into the boat. The baby had died. She said "How is it I cannot drown myself without the child?" She told Seddon that she had "been going out of her mind" for 3 weeks.

Seddon and Alps called for PC William Murray. He found Mooney with the baby in her arms. He wrapped his cape around them both and took them to Ancoats Hospital. When they got there she told him: "I have tried to poison myself and I ca not do that. I have tried to drown myself, and I cannot do that." Later that morning he charged her with wilful murder; she said "it was myself I meant, and not the child".

The baby was sent to the mortuary from the hospital. Her husband found out about this at 7:30am. An inquest was held on November 21st by deputy City coroner Sidney Smelt at the City Coroner's Court. Her husband said she had been acting strangely for about a month, but described her as "very temperate". He said he had never quarrelled with her, and they were very happy together.

Seddon said he had seen her at the foot of the canal bridge on the corner at Union Street, 10 minutes before hearing a shout and a splash.
Her neighbour, Mrs. Curran, said that on the night of November 17th Mooney had complained to her about a funny feeling in her head and admitted wanting to be dead. She said Mooney had bought some laudanum 3 weeks ago.

Hospital medical officer Arthur Emery said John was dead on arrival from drowning. He could not definitely diagnose Mooney's alleged insanity, but said that she seemed to be getting worse while she was in hospital. He said she had not been in long enough for him to comment properly. A verdict of wilful murder was returned, and she was committed on the Coroner's warrant to trial at the Assizes in the hopes that doctors would, by then, come to some decision as to her mental state. Later that day the Coroner's evidence was repeated before the magistrates, who agreed with the verdict and similarly committed her to the Assizes.

She was visited on November 22nd by Dr. Edwards of Strangeways Gaol. He said she was suffering melancholia and hallucinations which terrified her and made her life miserable. She was physically and mentally restless and had very little attention span. Her memory was very poor. He signed a certificate with Dr. Paton, sending her to an asylum with the instruction that she be under constant care.

She was discharged from Prestwich Asylum in February 1895. She appeared before Mr Justice Lawrance on March 1st, 1895, with Mr. Foard prosecuting and Royds defending her. Foard opened by pointing out that the case hinged upon whether Mooney was insane or not. Under the direction of the Secretary of State, a certificate, which was forwarded to the Home Office, was produced by two doctors of Prestwich Asylum attesting to her insanity at the time. This was corroborated by Dr. Rooke Ley of the Asylum.

He said she had gradually recovered during her stay there. Royds stated that Mooney was obviously hallucinating and delusional when she jumped into the canal. It was decided she actually was insane, and she was duly discharged with a verdict of "not guilty".

45.
THE WATCHMAKER'S DELUSION
30 Mar 1895

New Orleanian watchmaker Arthur Eisen (34) lived at 60 Great Ancoats Street, running his own shop. He had separated from his wife Emma, whom he had left in London about 11 years ago. He had begun to believe paid spies were watching him, planning to hurt him and drive him out of Manchester. One of these alleged spies was John Shepherd (50), a joiner who lived in Newgate, off Corporation Street. He went to the house at 6:00pm on a Saturday night. He said he wanted to speak to him. Shepherd asked what about; he said "you know." "I do not." "Will you have a drink?" He declined.

"I want you to speak the truth, and if you do not you'll have to die". "What am I to speak the truth about?" They quarrelled in the street for a few minutes, and were interrupted by Shepherd's friend, a pork butcher named Zeltner. Shepherd took the butcher to a mussels shop on Corporation Street, owned by James Parker.

Eisen followed them, but kept on the footpath. On the doorstep of the hut, Eisen asked Shepherd "will you tell me?". He did not, so Eisen shot Shepherd in the chest with a revolver. The bullet made a wound near the left collarbone, missing his coat and vest. It hit the ground, leading Shepherd to believe he had lost a button. Parker and Zeltner heard Shepherd's cry and rushed to apprehend Eisen. Zeltner said "My God, what have you done that for?!"
Eisen said "He's got it right enough".

Parker also asked why he had done it; he said "I know what I have done; I shall not run away". Eisen told them he would wait for a policeman, and urged them not to worry. At 6:30pm, PC Herbert Dorricott saw a crowd gathering opposite 124 Corporation

Street. He heard of the incident, and saw Eisen in the men's charge. Shepherd pointed to him and said "that man has shot me with a revolver". He was taken into custody at the station on Derby Street. On the way there, he was given over to PC Cook; Dorricott caught a cab to take Shepherd to the Infirmary.

The loaded revolver was seized from Eisen, who seemed to be genuinely concerned for Shepherd's health. He was drunk when he was arrested, and he was charged with attempted murder at 12:45am on March 31st. He said "I have been driven to it by Mr. Shepherd. I have been told he has been receiving money from my wife to pay loafers to hound me. I did not wish to hurt anyone. I could not get any satisfaction." The revolver contained 6 chambers, 5 loaded with one spent cartridge. He also had £2 16s. 4½d., a gold ring, two German silver watches, 8 ladies' watches, 5 door keys, 2 pawn tickets and a gold guard. He told Dorricott, who charged him, that the revolver was bought that day, or the day before.

Despite doctors initially doubting his recovery, Shepherd was well enough the next day for doctors to allow him to briefly attend the trial at the City Police Court on the morning of April 1st. The trial was held before Alderman Anthony Marshall and H Matthews. Eisen was represented by solicitor Mr. Harris. His many watches were brought into question by the court, and explained away by Harris. Harris asked that the trial be adjourned until April 5th, as he had only been informed of the case that morning and needed to talk more with Eisen, who was in a padded room and straitjacket at Strangeways.

He was duly remanded. Some time later that day, a woman came to Marshall and Matthews and told them that she had known Eisen for 12 months, and had talked to him on the morning of the incident; he had sounded insane. Two men also appeared and said that the watches found on Eisen belonged to other people. (He was found not guilty of stealing a watch in 1887). The magistrates told them to come back on April 5th.

On April 5th, Dorricott's evidence was repeated. Shepherd said that he had known Eisen for 18 months. He told the court that the bullet had not been found, and he did not know Eisen's wife. He had heard first-hand of Eisen's paranoia about a year before, and 'pooh-poohed' the idea that men were hounding him out of the city. He had last seen Eisen at Christmas 1894, and always thought he was a very nice man.

His apparent madness was corroborated by Alice Greenwood (Rochdale Road), a greengrocer who had known Eisen some time, and had seen him acting strangely on the day of the incident. Thomas Pretty had known Eisen for 23 years, and quarrelled with him a year prior over his delusions. He was committed to the Assizes.

He was admitted to Prestwich Asylum on the order of the Secretary of State on April 15th, and remained in there for at least another 16 years. He died in 1924.

46.

THE BIRCH BROOK BABY
12 Jul 1895

The body of a newly-born baby boy was found by a group of lads playing at Birch Brook, Rusholme on a Friday afternoon. It was partly enveloped in brown paper, with marks and bruises that suggested death from suffocation or strangulation. PC Yarwood took the body to the station on Monmouth Street, where police surgeon Richard Jessop Dearden (174 Oxford Road) conducted a post-mortem examination. An inquest was held on July 15th by deputy City coroner Sidney Smelt at the City Coroner's Court; the jury returned a verdict of wilful murder.

47.
THE MURDER AT THE STATION
7 Aug 1895

Labourer Tom Brooks (55), of Stourbridge, Worcestershire, turned up drunk at his wife Elizabeth and daughter's house of 89 Edensor Street, Beswick at about noon on August 6th, a Tuesday. It was his son-in-law, Thomas Gilbert's house; Brooks was estranged from his wife for 10 weeks, since ending a 17-day stay at Crumpsall Workhouse Asylum. She would not let him stay at the house due to his past violent behaviour, which was often caused by jealousy.

It was unclear what exactly his occupation was; he wrote many letters to her, mostly insulting and mean, but some told ridiculous tales of what he was up to. He left the house, and came back the next day at 6:30am. He hung around the doors for a while, then went away.

That evening he met his daughter Mary Ann (14) in Beswick as she walked home from work with friends. He asked her to walk to Phillip's Park Road with him, but she refused. He turned up at their house later on and said he was going back to Stourbridge, and Mary asked to accompany him. According to Gilbert, he looked quiet and comfortable, but his eyes sparkled with wildness.

They set off at 8:30pm; on the way to London Road train station they met Mrs. Brooks. The three of them arrived at the station at 8:40pm, and sat on Platform 3. They chatted for a quarter hour, and he asked them if they would visit him in Stourbridge. His daughter said she would, and she would save up her wages to afford the ticket. Brooks said he needed to buy his ticket from the office, and that his brother could get him one on account of being an employee there.

His wife asked him where he would get his ticket; he pointed to a door marked "private" and said it was in there. He was very calm at that time, and said "I will go now and get my pass". Mary said "I will go with you". Mrs. Brooks watched them go towards the door, then they disappeared. She started to walk towards the entrance of the station, then heard her daughter scream "Mama! Mama!". She ran towards the screams, and caught her daughter in her arms as she staggered out of the toilets on the corner of Platforms 3 and 4; she said "Oh, he's cut her throat!". Mary, quickly dying, pressed her shawl tightly against her throat.

Joseph Simms, a newspaper messenger, was at the station at 8:50pm, and saw Mary staggering about, shouting "Mama! Mama!". He saw Elizabeth come up to her and ask what was to do; according to him she replied "Dada", but did not accuse her father. That was when she caught her, and said "Oh, he's cut her throat". He helped to place her in John Baines' (Rochdale Road) milk float, and she was taken to the Infirmary.

A cabman, Walter Gatward (4 Granby Place), was stood in the cab rank of the station, and witnessed this. He had seen Brooks run or walk out of the station toilets and throw something on the ground. He had heard the scream and knew something was wrong. He got off his cab and picked the item up; it was a bloodstained butcher's knife. He followed Brooks down towards Piccadilly, and on the way informed PC Walker of what had happened.

Walker found Brooks walking quietly, and arrested him; he did not protest. He was taken into custody at the station on Fairfield Street.
JE Platt, a surgeon at the Infirmary said there was no hope for her upon admission at 9:40pm, and she died at 10:00pm. The item Brooks had thrown on the ground was found, and identified as a bloodstained butcher's knife; the sheath was found on his person.

Brooks was charged by Walker with wilful murder; he said nothing, but shook his head. Police inquiries, including those of Sgt Harney, could not conclude that the knife had been bought in Manchester; it seemed he had brought it with him from Stourbridge. Police suspected from the start that he was not of sound mind.

He appeared before stipendiary magistrate Francis John Headlam the next day at the City Police Court.

He was a short, mild- and inoffensive-looking man who sat on one of the side benches in the well of the court, his hands deep in his pockets, watching over the trial with an indifferent expression. He defended himself; he asked Walker if had found any blood on his clothes upon his arrest, which he did not. He probably asked Blackmore if he saw Mary's injuries; he did not, because he never took his eyes off Brooks after seeing him throw the knife down. He was remanded until August 9th, the day of the inquest.

The inquest was held by Louis J Aitken, acting deputy City coroner, at the City Coroner's Court. Aitken asked him why he was representing himself; he said he could not afford a solicitor. He acted entirely apathetic throughout the inquest, but seemed to focus very hard on specific bits of evidence. His wife was the first witness; she entered weeping bitterly, and he sneered and smiled mockingly at her. She explained how her husband loved their daughter, but was prone to fits of madness where he would threaten the girl with drowning and murder. Aitken asked how he had got discharged from the asylum; she said "I cannot tell; it's never been understood yet".

Brooks said he had one short question to ask his wife, but she had told a lot of lies in her statement. Aitken said "never mind that, ask her what question you want to ask her". He asked her: "Since Christmas, how many times have you had that girl used for immoral purposes to suit your ways?". His wife denied this. Aitken asked Mrs. Brooks what she meant; she explained her daughter was a virgin, and Brooks was just accusing her to make her look bad. Aitken said "Never mind that", and she raised her hand to her husband and said "Oh, you wretch!"

He asked Gatward if he had seen him leaving the toilets; when he answered "yes", Brooks said "You are mistaken; I was never in the lavatory. Do you think I would take her into the lavatory in broad daylight? But, I will have to take your answer".

Robert Arnold, a London and Northwestern Railway Company employee, said he had seen Brooks and Mary on the platform. He heard Brooks say "Polly, I must have some tonight". "You cannot, because we have not got it". "You must get it".

Platt said that Mary was badly wounded in the throat and back, and had been stabbed behind the left ear through to the throat in the back of her chin. There was a cut on her left ear, on her left shoulder and 5 on her back. There was a wound between her ribs and through her lung into her neck. There were 10 incised wounds in total. Considerable force was required for some of these. The death was attributed to shock and loss of blood. Brooks asked Platt if he had conducted the post-mortem; Platt confirmed this, and was asked if he had seen any evidence that Mary was not a virgin. He said he had not, and Brooks said "if you swear that, I must take your word for it".

Aitken committed Brooks to the Assizes on a charge of wilful murder. Later that day he appeared before Headlam again. He refuted Gatward's claim he had seen him leave the toilets; he asserted he had never even been in the toilets, but did confess to throwing away the knife.

Baines said that he had heard the screams coming from the toilets, and saw her pressing her hands and shawl against her throat. He corroborated Simms' claim that she did not implicate her father in the attack, and heard Mrs. Brooks' exclamation; but, he did not see Brooks at all. His lad, Thomas Lindley, corroborated his story.

Gilbert, who identified Mary's body, was asked if he had any questions for Brook; he said "No, I will not look at him". Brooks said "it is the last witness and his mother-in-law that is the cause of it. That is all I have to say here. What I have to say I will say in another place. There is one question I would like to ask; why has not Mrs. Brooks been called here to give evidence? She is the principal witness". Headlam said "she's your wife, and cannot give evidence against you". "Thank you, sir, that's all". He was similarly committed to the Assizes.

At the Manchester Assizes on November 4th, Mr. Overend Evans said he had made an application to decide whether to present a bill to the Grand Jury regarding the case. Brooks was in Prestwich Asylum since September 14th. Mr. Justice Kennedy said this was not a good idea at that exact time, but might be better later on.

48.
THE UNFAITHFUL WIFE
15 Aug 1895

Thomas Maddocks, a labourer of Parkgate, near Nelson, knew William Henry Beaumont (33), a Corporation labourer, for 23 years, and his wife Elizabeth (36), a mill reeler, since their marriage 8 years before. The Beaumonts lived at 150 Cheltenham Street, Collyhurst. Maddocks had been writing to them both, especially Elizabeth; he started the letters with "Dear Eliza". He visited the Beaumonts on August 14th, and stayed at the house that night. He took Elizabeth to see Beaumont at his work in Crumpsall on the morning of August 15th, where they all drank together in his lunch hour. Beaumont went back to work, and Maddocks and Elizabeth drank more, then went home and were "guilty of misconduct" that afternoon.

They had thought Beaumont would be home at 6:00pm as usual, but he came home at 3:00pm due to feeling unwell. He tried the door, but it was locked, so he went to his neighbour Agnes Craven (139 Cheltenham Street) for a key. He knocked twice, but nobody answered, so he went to another house to get a key. He went in and caught his wife in bed, with Maddocks leaving the bedroom. He asked them accusingly what they were doing, but Maddocks denied anything had been going on. Beaumont began shouting and swearing at his wife, and Maddocks ran away, caught a tram to the train station and got home to Nelson. They had been at this for about three months before then.

At 4:30pm their only daughter, Elizabeth (12) came home from school to find Beaumont sitting in the kitchen smoking. She asked for her mother, and he told her she was sleeping upstairs. This was verified by the girl. About 6:30pm Beaumont went upstairs and smacked his wife, making her cry. Later that night, Beaumont told the daughter her mother had been doing something wrong, and told her to wash some dirty handkerchiefs. At about 9:00pm he beat up his wife to the point at which she died from the injuries. He called out to his daughter: "your mamma is dead; it is a good job for me." He then went to a neighbour's house and told them Elizabeth had died suddenly in bed next to him. He claimed he had gone to sleep with her at 7:00pm, woken up at 9:30pm, and found her dead. He claimed she was drunk and had fallen down the stairs three times.

He fetched a doctor, Dr. Hubert Arthur E Noble, and then informed police at the Willert Street station. PC Robert Davies attended the scene and saw Elizabeth dead in bed, badly bruised and clearly murdered. He asked Beaumont to explain what had happened, and he gave a long rambling statement that Davies found suspicious. He took Beaumont into custody, and charged him with murder the next night. A statement was given. He appeared at the City Police Court before Sir RT Leach and other magistrates on August 17th. He had no questions to ask and no statement to make, and was remanded until August 19th.

Later that day the acting deputy Coroner, Louis J Aitken, opened the inquest at the City Coroner's Court. Beaumont appeared, represented by solicitor WF Alderson. Elizabeth Jones (900 Rochdale Road, Collyhurst), Mrs. Beaumont's aunt and stepmother, told the court they had been married 8 years. She said she did not much like Beaumont, and so had not talked to him or her stepdaughter for about a year. She described Mrs. Beaumont as a "steady woman". She was sent for after the incident, and agreed it was clear there was some violence used against her. She said Mrs. Beaumont had complained to her of domestic abuse 2 years before, but nothing had come out of it. She had gone to Jones' house two or three times to escape her husband's violence.

Mrs. Eyeres (146 Cheltenham Street) said she saw labourer Thomas Maddocks, of Parkgate, near Nelson, leave

Beaumont's house on August 15th. A few minutes later she heard the sound of blows coming from their bedroom, followed by Beaumont telling her to "get up!". Maddocks was a frequent visitor, and had once spent a three-week holiday there. The Beaumonts got on well with him; their daughter called Maddocks "Uncle", but he was not related.

Maddocks was then called upon. The Coroner brought up that in these letters, he would start them "Dear Eliza". He asked whether Beaumont knew about these letters; Maddocks said he knew about them, and read them sometimes. He said he had written a few, but had not kept count, and "believed" she had replied to them sometimes. He had burnt the letters she had sent to him. He said he had also written to Beaumont. He gave his account of the case and his escape from the house. The foreman juror said "you were glad to get away".

Noble said he believed Mrs. Beaumont had been dead some hours when he was brought to the house. He saw bruises on her face, and Beaumont again gave his account of the event. He appeared to be slightly drunk. Agnes Craven (139 Cheltenham Street) said Beaumont had knocked at her door twice on the afternoon of August 15th, but nobody answered. He borrowed a key from a neighbour and went into his house.

Dr Smith had conducted the post-mortem examination. There was no blood on the body, but her face, hands, arms and other parts had clearly been washed. There were 19 bruises on her head and face. There were 5 bruises on her forehead and temple and 5 under her chin. Her eyes were black, and there was a bruise on the bridge of her nose and more on her ears. The skin on the tip of her nose was gone. The inner surface of her lips were lacerated; the lower lip was lacerated in three lines. There were 11 marks on her right arm, and a virtually continuous bruise from her elbow to the back of her hand. Her left arm was badly bruised, and 6 bruises covered her upper arm. Her left arm was marked as if she had been kicked by a boot, with 3 bruises on her chest and one on each side of her body. There were large bruises on her buttocks and 14 marks on her legs. The whole front of the right shin was bruised, with an effusion of blood suggesting strangulation by the throat. Two of her ribs on the right side were broken near the spine. He decided the death was due to shock from the severe injuries. Alderson proposed the broken ribs was caused by a fall downstairs.

Aitken said that Beaumont had "received one of the greatest wrongs a man could receive" due to the sheer number of wounds he had inflicted on his wife, and the wounds suggested the violence had been going on for some time. This was the difference between a verdict of manslaughter (an act of passion) and of wilful murder. He asked Smith how many blows Beaumont had dealt her; he estimated it to be between 70 and 80.

After 10 minutes of deliberation, the jury returned a verdict of manslaughter. Alderson advised Beaumont not to say anything, and he was committed to the Assizes. That afternoon he was brought before stipendiary magistrates, including Francis John Headlam, at the City Police Court, represented by Alderson. Davies gave a statement that he and Inspector Hewitt had searched the house after hearing Beaumont's statement. He claimed he had punched her in the face once after catching her with Maddocks. Davies presented various bloodstained items in court, and mentioned finding blood on the bedroom wallpaper and a letter from Maddocks to Mrs. Beaumont, saying that he would visit her after finishing his haymaking in Clapham. Beaumont's statement, made on August 16th, was read out.

"I came home from my work on Thursday. I did not feel very grand. I knocked at the door, and got no answer. I got a key from next door and went in. I looked round, and then went upstairs and found her in bed with Thomas Maddocks, and then we had a fight, and he took his hook and ran downstairs. She was drunk, and I tried to get her into bed, and she fell downstairs twice. I then laid her on the side of the bed to quieten her. I then fell asleep, and wakened between half-past eight and nine. I thought she

was dead, and sent for the doctor, and then I gave information to Willert Street police station."

He was committed to the Assizes on a charge of wilful murder. On November 5th, he appeared at the Manchester Crown Court before Mr. Justice Kennedy. He was prosecuted by Mr. Jordan and Mr. McNab, and Charles Pilling McKeand defended him. Maddocks was cross-examined by McKeand, and called himself a "labourer in connection with drain work" and also a betting man. He said Elizabeth was not drunk that night, and that he had drunk "about as much as [he] could carry". He also denied that Beaumont caught them in the act or that Beaumont hit him; for some reason Beaumont rose from his seat in the dock and said "tell the truth, Tom", but Maddocks did not change his story.

McKeand pleaded for a manslaughter sentence based on Beaumont's 'excellent character', based on the fact he had never stood in a dock before, but the judge declined to pass sentence that day, apparently on account of not hearing medical evidence. The trial commenced on November 7th, with Kennedy having "most anxiously and carefully perused the evidence" surrounding the murder.

It appears Beaumont had already pleaded guilty on the advice of his defence. He took into account that adultery would provide Beaumont, legally, with "very grave provocation", but the delay between the adultery and murder was such a length of time that it could not be called a crime of passion. He was sentenced to 7 years' penal servitude for manslaughter.

49.
THE WIFE PUSHER

24 Aug 1895

Sidney Brearley pushed his wife Annie over on a Saturday on Thomas Street, Miles Platting. Her head hit the flags, and her skull fractured. She died the same day. An inquest was held by acting Deputy Coroner Louis J Aitken on August 26th, and an open verdict was returned. It seemed to be the belief of the majority of the jury that the death was accidental. Police arrested Brearley at the Shudehill fish market, where he worked as a porter, later that week in connection with the death.

He was brought before stipendiary magistrates F Milne and JD Milne at the City Police Court on August 30th, and remanded until September 4th, when he appeared before Mr. Furniss and Mr. Parlane. He was committed to the Assizes. He then appeared before Mr. Justice Kennedy at the Manchester Crown Court on November 2nd, prosecuted by Mr. Foard and defended by Mr. Jordan. A verdict of not guilty was returned.

50.
THE DANCER'S FINALE
16 Oct 1895

Elaine Murray "Nellie" Rourke (38, nee Goodman) poisoned herself and her two children at their home of 60 Nelson Street, Manchester on a Tuesday night. She was a well-known professional dance teacher who went by "Madame Elene Webster", and lived with her husband Charles Joseph, a cotton waste merchant, and their sons Kenneth ("Kennie", 8) and the son of her previous husband, (Stephen) William Hilton Webster (11).

Her husband came home at 7:00pm or 8:00pm. She complained to him of feeling unwell all day, and appeared despondent. At 8:30pm he kissed her and the boys, leaving them in the boys' bedroom. She seemed to be agitated by his presence (as she often did), so he went back out again, and around 10:00pm their servant heard strange moaning noises coming from the bedroom. She went in and found Elaine, Kennie and William in bed, nearly unconscious. Rourke returned, and was told by the servant that Elaine was asleep and snoring heavily.

He could smell drug fumes from downstairs, and went to the bedroom to see two gas jets fully on, but not lit. He spoke to her, but she did not take any notice; he grabbed his wife's shoulders and said "Nell, what have you done? What have you given to the children and taken yourself?" She responded: "Why disturb us? We are all passing peacefully away". The servant fetched the family doctor, Dr. John Prince Stallard (Oxford Street), who arrived at 10:00pm and diagnosed narcotic poisoning. He gave them emetics to vomit out the poison, and Kennie survived, but Stephen died soon after.

Elaine was made well enough to walk, but died the next day at 3:00am. She had received artificial respiration most of the time between the poisoning and her death. Police were informed, and plain-clothes detectives Wesley Ernest Cubberley and Charles Broomfield were sent to inquire. They searched the bedroom and found two chlorodyne bottles, and another containing a drop of chloral. Under the bed was a cup that smelt of chlorodyne. Kennie had just recovered enough to be able to talk; he told the detectives that his mother had given him medicine, apparently for a cold.

He told her he did not have a cold, and she said the "stuff" would put him to sleep. She had written three suicide notes, which were found by her brother on the bedside table.

The one to her husband read, in part:
"If I could have taken my girls I would. Be gentle and good to them all, for God's sake. Your desperate and hopeless Nell."
To a former servant she wrote:
"Dear Nurse, no-one but you is to touch one of us. You know where to find everything. You have been so good to me. Do come after me. Your loving mistress."
And to her brother:
"One last line. God bless you (if there is a God). Your unhappy sister, Nellie."
The girls mentioned in the letter to her husband were at a boarding school in Sale. She had sent a servant in a cab to fetch them, and the murder had already been committed by the time the servant arrived.

The inquest was held on October 18th by deputy City coroner Sidney Smelt at the City Coroner's Court. HT Crofton (Crofton & Craven) watched the inquest on Rourke's behalf, while solicitor Mr. Jordan appeared on behalf of her brother Archie Webster. A man told Smelt that Ellen was married to a WH Webster, who had died, and Archie assumed the name, for some reason.

Rourke said he "understood" his wife's strange moods, and did not think she was insane. He said she had taken some sort of medicine that day, either chloral or chlorodyne. She had been taking this every day for a long time. Under the influence of this medicine she was irritable, and his presence seemed to agitate her; but he had never quarrelled with her and was determined not to. That was why he had left.

The suicide notes were not read at the inquest by the Coroner's request. He noticed from the letters that one of the issues in Mrs. Rourke's life was money troubles. Mr. Rourke attested to these, but Jordan claimed that Webster told him the money troubles were virtually non-existent. Rourke said that in January he had asked his wife how she stood financially, and "she would be put straight to a penny piece" by him. The problem grew and then stopped, but had troubled her immensely.

Stallard said that Mrs. Rourke had had a breast removal operation due to cancer in 1892, but other than that was perfectly fine physically. She was excitable and nervous, but never so much as hinted that she would kill herself or hurt her children. A juror asked if she had ever made any threats; Mr. Rourke said she had once threatened to kill herself, when she had cancer. A verdict of murder through temporary insanity was returned against Mrs. Rourke.

51.
THE FALSE SPIRIT OF CHORLTON
26 Oct 1895

Edward Clegg (38), an engine belt weaver or hosepipe maker, came home to 66 Lower Cambridge Street, Chorlton-on-Medlock at about 7:00pm on a Saturday night, and saw his wife, Georgina, with a horse-shoer, Fred Naylor. They had a row, and he kicked them out; she came back later with another woman, and the row started up again. She threw his hat on the fire, and "a false spirit came over him and he hit her". She was taken to the Infirmary, where she remained in a very serious condition for a few days. She had 5 wounds on the back of her head and a compound fracture on her skull.

At 1:30am the next morning he visited her at the hospital, and was arrested by Detective Sgts. Cubberley and Bloomfield. He had known Bloomfield for many years, and told him his story; he claimed an "evil spirit" had possessed him, and he did not know what had happened. The last thing he remembered was seeing blood on the fender. He said he had had some drink, but was not drunk.

Clegg was brought before stipendiary magistrates Bannerman and Austin at the City Police Court on October 28th on a charge of grievous bodily harm. Cubberley produced the hatchet used in the attack, which was covered in blood and hair, and had been found by PC Edwards. In order to get Mrs. Clegg's statement, he was remanded until October 30th, when he was remanded again.

He appeared, looking very ill, before magistrates Evans and Pritchard on November 27th, and was given a seat in the dock. His wife, who was bandaged and still a patient at the Infirmary, feebly declared that her husband had been aggressive and violent for some years, in the hopes of making her "a better woman".

Bloomfield told the court that Clegg had complained to him several times before about his wife. Dr. Platt appeared, from the Infirmary, to attest to Mrs. Clegg's poor condition after the attack. Mrs. Clegg had difficulty in giving her statement, but said that she was at work in the day and came home with her wages. She found Clegg was not home yet, and set about cleaning the house. He got home at 8:00pm, and later on Naylor called "on business". Clegg pushed Naylor outside, and she went to a neighbour's house.

When she got back, he was burning a picture frame. He swore at her, and almost knocked her out with the hatchet. She was cross-examined by her husband, who sought to prove her infidelity; she denied this, but admitted she had been imprisoned for a month for child neglect, and an inquest had been held on one of their children found dead in bed. A neighbour, Daisy Kind, said she was passing the house on the night of the attack, and saw through the window Clegg holding an axe above his head. She watched him leave the house, unlock the door and go up Devonshire Street.

Naylor was called; he said he knew Mrs. Clegg for 18 months, and had never met Clegg before that night. He had procured some things from Mrs. Clegg through the hire system, and that was why he was there that night. She had invited him in, and he saw Clegg lying on the sofa. When Clegg asked him his business, he felt it unwise to tell him. This was when Clegg became enraged and began to push him. He and Mrs. Clegg fell out onto the street; he picked himself up and went to his club on Great Jackson Street. Clegg also questioned Naylor in court; his answers showed that he had lived with Mrs. Clegg on Morton Street, Longsight before she got married, and had slept together at the house on Lower Cambridge Street. Mrs. Clegg adamantly denied this, and accused Naylor of being drunk. Clegg was committed to trial at the Assizes.

He pleaded guilty at the Assizes on December 11th; the Recorder, Mr. Lecse, said he had no doubt that Clegg had severe provocation, but not enough to justify the barbaric assault. Taking this into consideration, and his ill health, he was given 6 months imprisonment without hard labour for unlawful wounding.

52.
GOSSIP ABOUT THE BOSS
27 Nov 1895

John Taylor (50) lived with his lodger, Londoner George Duncan (54) on Chapel Street, Levenshulme; they were employed as cobblers at the same firm. At 8:00am on a Wednesday morning, in their home, they quarrelled over their boss' wife. Duncan had told their boss about Taylor's conduct the previous night, and that morning told Taylor he would tell the boss what he had said about his wife. Taylor said "What the hell has it got to do with you?" Taylor hit Duncan in the left breast while he was cutting tobacco with a shoemaker's knife. He "forgot" he was holding the knife and stabbed Taylor in the neck. Duncan put on his hat, ran out the back door and tramped to Poynton before people started to gather. Taylor ran out of the house, shouting "Murder!".

Neighbours tried to help, but he collapsed and died at 8:45am. County Constables from the division were sent to search for Duncan under the personal supervision of Superintendent Bent, who also brought in outside help. 6 people who knew Duncan were also sent in various directions, and the entire division was scoured. Meanwhile Duncan visited an acquaintanced shoemaker in Poynton, Henry Johnson, and asked for employment. Johnson could not find him any work, and advised him to walk to New Mills and Marple, 5 miles away.

Between 30 and 60 minutes later he returned to Poynton and confessed the murder to Johnson. Johnson advised him to give himself up, so they went to the police station. He asked Sgt. William Maddocks there if he had heard of the assault in Levenshulme; he said he had not. He confessed to the crime, and apparently did not know he had murdered Taylor. He was detained until Inspector Pattison, one of Bent's men, went and heard Duncan's statement, then took him to Old Trafford. There he was charged with murder and gave another statement. He was described by the *Manchester Courier* as being "somewhat eccentric in his manner".

He was brought before stipendiary magistrate J Yates, Q.C., at the County Police Court on the morning of November 29th on a murder charge. Inspector Cameron read Duncan's statement, and Bent said an inquest would be held later that day purely to identify the body. He asked for a remand, and was granted one until December 5th. At the inquest, he was committed for trial at the Assizes.

On December 5th he appeared again before Yates, and other magistrates, prosecuted by Mr. Brookes. He did not call any witnesses. He said "I want to speak, but I cannot speak here without a lawyer, or some assistance. I got great aggravation for what I did, and I am not sorry for what I did to him. I was knocked down, and I was in peril of my life. He struck me and knocked me down". Yates asked "you want a lawyer to speak for you?". He said, "there must be someone; I cannot speak for myself". He was committed to the Assizes on a charge of wilful murder.

He appeared before Mr. Justice Vaughan Williams at the Manchester Crown Court on February 22nd, 1896.

Among the Grand Jury was Sir WH Houldsworth, Baronet of Reddish, and Lord Mayor AE Lloyd. Williams informed the jury that there was some doubt as to Duncan's sanity, but to only consider this at the time of the trial. Mr. Foard and McKeand appeared for the prosecution. Drs. Paton and Ley, of Strangeways Gaol and Prestwich Asylum respectively, gave testimonies as to Duncan's hallucinations and delusions. He was not fit to stand trial, and they believed his illness to be permanent. He was returned to custody, and from there put into Prestwich Asylum. He died there in 1916.

53.
THE CHORLTON STREET WAREHOUSE
29 Dec 1895

Before giving the details of this convoluted case, it is important to introduce the key 'characters', and their confirmed whereabouts at the time of the murder.

1. Maud Moore, a 34-year-old prostitute lodging at 6 Lower Chatham Street, Chorlton-on-Medlock, the victim.
2. Elizabeth Ann Riley, another prostitute living on Angel Street, Rochdale Road, and a friend of Moore's, who was walking about nearby.
3. Robert Stainforth, the manager of a warehouse on Chorlton Street, and employer of John Rowbottom, who was at home.
4. Annie Freeman, another prostitute living with Riley, who was also walking about.
5. John "Jack" Rowbottom, a 40-year-old man and the initial suspect, a firer-up at Stainforth's warehouse and habitual client of local prostitutes, including Freeman and Wharton. He took both women into the warehouse in the past. He found the body with other men.
6. William "Billy" Mitchell, a young man living off Collyhurst Street. He found the body with other men.
7. Mary Ellen Craig, another prostitute living with Moore, who was also walking about.
8. Matilda Wharton, another prostitute living on Charter Street, who knew Rowbottom. She was walking about.
9. Leonard Lomas, a police constable who was called to the scene by Rowbottom.
10. Henry Key, an engineer's labourer at the warehouse, living on Eliza Street, City Road. He was a married man and father of two, with a wife dying from consumption. He was 5' 6", a "big man in a little compass", short and stout.

Key was seen by various people having a fight in a pub in the city at about 7:00pm on Saturday night, December 28th. Moore happened to be one of those people. He was seen outside another pub just after 9:00pm. Between 9:00pm and 10:00pm he took Moore into the warehouse, using a key belonging to the engineer, Clark. He had had to argue for the key. He told Clark he would give the key back the same day, but did not return it until 6:00pm on January 1st. Four keys had gone missing in the last few months. Every department had its own key due to the amount of overtime necessary; the business required imported packages to be prepared immediately, so the warehouse had to be ready to be opened at any time.

Key further claimed he went into the toilets in the cellar, but she did not follow him, so he went back to the warehouse to find her. He left the warehouse hurriedly, witnessed by someone living opposite.

Moore and Riley were on Bloom Street at about 6:00pm on a Sunday evening. Two men (a tall one and a short one) came up and propositioned them. They said they could access Robert Stainforth's warehouse at 40 Chorlton Street.

Riley refused them, but Moore accepted, saying she knew the warehouse well. She tried to convince Riley to accompany her, but she declined. Moore went away with the men, and Riley watched them turning into Sackville Street, then left the scene. Freeman was on Chorlton Street at about 6:25pm. She saw firer-up John Rowbottom (whom she knew as "Jack") opening the warehouse door and going in, followed by Moore, whom she did not know. She later saw a light shining from a window above the door.

At about 6:35pm, Rowbottom went into the Ogden Arms on Sackville Street and said he was looking for a policeman.

He said there was an unknown person in his "shop". He asked if someone would come with him, and the 7 or 8 men there (including William "Billy" Mitchell, living off Collyhurst Street), all volunteered. When they got to the warehouse, Rowbottom unlocked the door and Mitchell struck a light. They saw Moore's clothes in the making-up room, and all grew frightened. A door was stuck shut, so 3 or 4 of the men got over a 3-feet high partition, followed by the others. They then heard Moore crying "Oh, master, I am here, do come this way." They found Moore half-naked on a bulkhead beside a water cistern, raised 4 feet off the ground.

Some of the men asked what she was doing there. She said she had met a man outside at 10:30pm the previous night, who had pushed her down a lift shaft, brought her back up again, and placed her on the platform, 20 yards from the shaft. Her black straw hat was found on one of the lift's cross beams. Mitchell gave her some brandy and arranged for her to be taken to the Infirmary. This was at about 7:10pm.

Freeman heard a policeman's whistle, and ran to the warehouse to see a gathering crowd. She was told a woman had been found inside; she said "Oh, no!". PC Leonard Lomas was informed by Rowbottom of Moore's appearance in the warehouse, and turned up with Rowbottom to inquire. He talked with Moore, but did not take much notice of what she was saying; he thought she was rambling. She kept saying her legs were broken, which he did not believe. Rowbottom was in the same room, but did not seem to hear Moore or Lomas. Lomas had Moore conveyed to the Infirmary, probably by Mitchell, and Freeman identified her as she was being removed. She died en route.

An inquest was held on December 31st by deputy City coroner Sidney Smelt, at the City Coroner's Court. Moore's co-lodger, Mary Ellen Craig, said she last saw Moore on the night of December 28th when they went out between 6:00pm and 7:00pm.

She was in good health and sober. Riley said she had known Moore for 11 years, and could not identify the men if she saw them again.

Annie Freeman (Angel Street) said she knew Rowbottom as a regular customer who had taken her to the warehouse several times, but did not know Moore. She said he was wearing a billycock hat. Smelt asked Rowbottom to stand up; Freeman said "Yes, that's the man". Smelt asked him to put on his hat, which Freeman confirmed was the same as the one worn on that night. Rowbottom said "I can contradict you on one thing; you say I lit the gas when I first went in."

Smelt said "No, she says that after you got inside she saw a light was shining through the window over the door".

"Will you state how long I was in?"

"I do not know", Freeman replied.

"I was not in four seconds. As to my being there between 6:20 and 6:30, I did not leave home until 6:30, and I had to come from Pin Mill Brow, Ardwick."

Riley was recalled, and said Rowbottom was nothing like the man who had propositioned her and Moore. Matilda Wharton (Charter Street) corroborated Freeman's story, and said Rowbottom had taken her into the warehouse twice before. She said she did not think it was actually Moore who had gone in, but definitively identified Rowbottom.

Superintendent Bannister said he could call witnesses to confirm that Moore was incorrect when she said she had been in the warehouse since Saturday night. Riley confirmed she was with Moore until 9:10pm on Saturday night, and was definitely with her on the night of the incident.

Dr JE Platt of the Infirmary said he had found 14 recent bruises on various parts of the body, but only two of them were particularly bad. Her breast bone was fractured, and her intestines were ruptured. The peritonitis from this injury was given as the cause of death, as well as shock. They corresponded with a fall from a high height. He said she must have lived two or three hours after the injuries were caused, but also gave 24 hours as a maximum. He did not say her legs were broken.

Rowbottom then gave a voluntary statement. He said he had left home at 6:30pm to light the fires at the warehouse for the next morning. When he got to the top of the warehouse stairs he heard a voice saying "Come this way, I am here", or "This is the road, master, I am here". He went out to find help, walking as far as Minshull Street to find a policeman. Not finding one, he walked past the warehouse again and saw a light in the cellar. He went to the Stockport Arms and talked to Sarah Wood, the landlady, and asked if she had seen anyone in the warehouse. She said she had not, but the light had been on in the cellar all evening. She said she had seen a man go in before; he said "that was me. I just went in, and I heard a groan, which sounded like a woman's voice." He then went to the Ogden Arms, hearing that Mitchell, a friend of his, was there. They found Moore, who told them she had been brought there by a stout man, with a dark moustache, brown cap and long overcoat.

PC Lomas said he had seen no evidence of a break-in; Rowbottom said he had lost a key four months ago. Stainforth was called upon, and said Rowbottom had been fired 3 or 4 times during his 4-year employment there for unsteadiness. He said Rowbottom, and 3 or 4 other men, held keys to the place, and that 3 or 4 keys were missing.

Rowbottom said his predecessor was a stout "sailor chap"; Stainforth said he was only working there a week, and would not have any keys. He said the engineer and a labourer, Henry Key, were there until 4:30pm on the Saturday afternoon, and the labourer would have taken a key home with him when he locked up. Whoever had opened the warehouse at 4:00am on Sunday morning would be the last person authorised to do so, and he would have a key.

At this point, Riley and another women were recalled and again verified it was Sunday, not Saturday, that the incident had taken place. Stainforth criticised police for not searching the warehouse thoroughly, a sentiment Smelt agreed with. His workers had found a muff in a room above the one Moore was found in.

Mrs. Wood corroborated what Rowbottom had told the inquest about her involvement in the incident. Smelt said he did not think the jury could come to a proper conclusion based on the evidence supplied, and adjourned the inquest until January 7th. Rowbottom appeared at the City Police Court later that day before Mr. Hughes and Horsfall, and was remanded until January 7th, bail being refused.

Under the direction of Chief Inspector Jerome Caminada, police began to find evidence suggesting Rowbottom's innocence; some sort of medical inspection supported this. Caminada and Inspector Hargreaves arrested Henry Key at the warehouse on January 2nd, telling him they were acting on a description supplied of a man who was seen near the warehouse around 9:00pm, and who left at 9:30pm. He kept saying he knew nothing about it. He said he was working in the warehouse on Saturday afternoon, then went to a nearby pub. Caminada told him they could place him in another nearby pub until 9:00pm the same night. They took him to the detective's office, where Caminada charged him. He initially made no reply, but later called Caminada back to give him a written statement:

"About 5 o'clock on the Saturday afternoon I left the warehouse, and got the key from the engineer. I went to the Ogdens' Arms, and had some drink, also the Mechanics' Arms, Chorlton Street, and had a good deal of drink. I came out of the Mechanics' Arms to go home about nine o'clock, and the

woman met me, and I took her to the warehouse and up the first flight of stairs. I then went into the cellar, and then came out of the warehouse and went straight home. I do not know what became of the woman. I do not remember seeing the woman after."

Rowbottom appeared at the City Police Court before RA Armitage again late in the afternoon on January 2nd. Chief Detective Inspector Jerome Caminada, under the direction of the Chief Constable, gave a statement that the police had taken Henry Key into custody. They found that Moore had been drunk in a pub that afternoon, and was probably taken there by the engineer and the labourer. They also believed her death was accidental.

Mitchell was called again, and confirmed Moore did not accuse Rowbottom. He said she might have been drunk, and she did ask for drink when they found her.

Another unnamed witness (possibly PC Lomas) said he was passing along Chorlton Street on the night of the incident, when he heard a whistle and went to the warehouse to find Moore. He asked her repeatedly who had done it, and she said a man had taken her there at 10:30pm on December 28th. Rowbottom was there but she did not accuse him. Rowbottom was released on a £5 bail to appear the next morning. Hughes and Horsfall received letters securing their attendance. Rowbottom thanked the bench and magistrate very much, and was choked up and sobbing.

The next morning Key appeared before Armitage at the City Police Court. He asked if it could be proved that Key had a key to the warehouse; Caminada confirmed this. Rowbottom surrendered to his bail, and was told by Armitage: "We have very much pleasure in discharging you. You leave the court without a stain on your character." Key was remanded until January 8th.

Smelt re-opened the inquest on January 8th at the City Coroner's Court. It was reported by the *Manchester Courier* that her legs were, in fact, broken. PH Jordan watched the inquest on Key's behalf, as Key 'refused' to show up. Smelt had written to the Governor of Strangeways Gaol to ask if Key could attend, and received a reply saying that Key simply did not want to come. It was, of course, not a question of whether Key wanted to be there or not.

He needed Key there to see if Riley could identify him as one of the two men (the tall and short men) that propositioned Moore. Riley's claim that she had last seen Moore as late as 6:00pm contradicted the doctor's evidence, which stated Moore must have received her injuries at 3:00pm at the latest. Riley was recalled, and said she last saw Moore at 5:20pm on the Sunday evening. She said, to the amusement of those present, that the man was "a big man, like a detective, tall and stout".

54.
THE BRICKLAYER'S BABY
2 Apr 1896

Bricklayer Joseph Hirst (26) murdered his illegitimate 12-month-old daughter by strangling it with a cord at his lodgings on York Street, Chorlton-on-Medlock. He tied the cord around its neck and, with the mother's help, threw the body into the Rochdale Canal at Ashton Old Road with a heavy stone attached to the child's waistband. He and the child's mother, factory hand or laundress Martha Ann Goddard (22), were arrested by Inspector Jerome Caminada in Leicester early in the morning on June 4th, and were taken to Manchester.

    They were brought before Mr Commissioner Dugdale, Q.C., at the Manchester Assizes on July 14th on a charge of murder; Goddard was charged with being an accessory. Joseph Leese, Q.C., M.P., and Mr. Byrne were counsel for the prosecution, while Hirst was defended by Mr. Cottingham and Goddard by B.G. Wilkinson. She pleaded not guilty immediately, and was discharged by Leese in order to be used as a witness for the prosecution and for cross-examination by Hirst. Leese did not believe there would be a strong case against her anyway.

    It was revealed that the couple had been living together for some months, and he was in the habit of abusing her and the baby. Cottingham's defence was that the baby's identification was poor evidence, and that Hirst had been denied his right to argue this evidence by the police. He confessed to acting alone, and claimed Goddard was acting under his influence. Cottingham said that a man who confessed to acting alone, was likely too good a man to commit murder. After 35 minutes' deliberation, during which a 'callous' Hirst talked with his counsel, the jury returned a verdict of guilty. Hirst said "I have nothing to say". The Commissioner said Hirst should "spend the days remaining to him in seeking the forgiveness of Almighty God", as the *Manchester Courier* put it. He was found guilty and executed on August 4th at Strangeways, after being visited several times by relatives.

55.
THE CLOUT AT HARPURHEY
12 Sep 1896

Sarah Hall (43) lived at 8 Staveley Street, Harpurhey with her husband, William (42), a "sober and reliable" carter of 3 years for the Manchester Corporation who worked nights. They occupied the 10ft-by-11ft front bedroom with their 21- and 10-year-old sons, 5-year-old daughter and 2-year-old infant. A 17-year-old daughter slept on the couch downstairs. They lodged with a couple, Louisa and Matthew Lynch, and their little girl and two other children, the eldest child being 11. They slept on a mattress in the back bedroom, which was entirely empty. The house was similarly barren, with sparse furniture downstairs but for a hen- and pigeon-coop in the back kitchen. They used the downstairs front room as a kitchen and dining area.

On about September 10th, the Halls received a school board summons for failing to send their children to school. She hid this from her husband, but he found out and fought with her about it. At about 9:15pm on a Saturday night, the Halls' daughter Mary Ann Atkins (34 Staveley Street) saw her mother walking away from Staveley Street, on Factory Lane. She had had some drink, but was not staggering; she had drunk at Atkins' house that morning.

He returned home from work early on a Saturday night, had some supper and went to bed before 10:00pm. Mrs. Lynch got home at 10:00pm. Ellen Moores (14 Staveley Street) went into the house at 10:30pm, and saw the Lynches and Mrs. Hall. The Lynches were drunk. Moores left at 11:10pm, then Lynch and her husband went to bed. Mrs. Hall came in very soon after; the Hall children were already in bed. The Lynch children then came in; they had been out drinking, and were singing.

They also went to bed, leaving Mrs. Hall the only one who was still up. At about 11:30pm one of the Lynches' daughters, Annie (10) woke her parents up to tell them she could hear the Halls fighting. Her mother put on a skirt and jacket and left the room to investigate, followed by Annie. At the top of the stairs she could hear Mrs. Hall saying "Do not be spiteful against me about the child, because I ca not make him go to school." She then went downstairs to find Mrs. Hall lying on the floor in the living room, with Mr. Hall stood against the cupboard or mantelpiece a few yards from her, holding a baby. Lynch raised Mrs. Hall's head; she said "Louisa, he has struck/pushed me", or "Louisa, hit/pushed".

She had a bad gash in the centre of her forehead, from the hairline to between her eyes. The door was open, and Lynch called for help. Hall said nothing more the entire night. Atkins was sent for at 11:20pm, and went to the house to see Mrs. Lynch trying to support her mother in her arms as she lay bleeding on the floor. There was a crowd gathering outside, and her father was just walking down the stairs. Lynch asked her to fetch a doctor, and she went. She apparently did not hear her mother or father speak, though claimed at the assizes she had asked her father what he had done; he said "I do not know". She went for a doctor, then used the poker on the fire and threw it on the sofa.

A neighbour, Catherine McCormick, was passing the house at 11:45pm. Through the open door she saw Lynch holding Hall up, saying "Oh dear, Sarah." McCormick tried to give Hall a drink of water, but it ran out of her mouth. Neighbours came to the house, woken by the commotion.

McCormick said "Dear, dear, she's dead. Will anybody run for a policeman or a doctor?" Dr. Dick arrived and found Mrs. Hall beyond hope, and she died quickly. PC Edward Godley came at 11:50pm and saw a badly-drunk Mr. Hall sitting with a baby on a chair, with his wife dead on the floor. A woman said "Oh, Mr. Hall, what have you done?".

He laughed and said "How do you know but what she's done it herself? I only gave her a clout and she fell". Godley told him it was a very serious affair, and the blood-soaked poker was found by PC William Willshaw behind Hall, on the sofa. He took it into the light and saw bloodstains on the knob end. He went back to Hall, who said "I gave her a *** thump", or "I only gave her one *** clout". Willshaw told him not to say anything further to incriminate himself. He arrested Hall, and took him to the nearby Moston Lane station. He said nothing, and finally made a statement the following night before being charged; the police were hesitant to charge him as they heard a lot of conflicting statements in evidence.

Sgt. Baird and PC Jackson were put in charge of the case. They found an 18" long poker in the house, with bloodstains on the thin end. It was also bent, though evidence suggested it was straight before the quarrel. It appeared the poker had been wiped clean of some blood. Baird and Jackson were "quite unprepared" for the state of the house when they searched it, despite being in such a rough area where squalor was very common. The police believed Hall to be "quiet, hardworking and temperate". The inquest was held by deputy City coroner Sidney Smelt at the City Coroner's Court on September 14th, the same day as the trial at the County Police Court.

The inquest was watched by Superintendent Smith for the police, while Hall represented himself. He laughed as he gave testimony and interrogated the witnesses called upon. Her daughter Mary Ann Atkins (34 Staveley Street) was first called. In response to the coroner, she said she did not know about any quarrel between her parents, but knew about the summons. Mrs. Lynch said she knew about the quarrel and the summons, and said Mr. Hall was not drunk, but was 'stupified'. She described Mrs. Hall as a heavy smoker and a lightweight alcoholic. She said it was her that told Mr. Hall about the summons on September 10th; apparently she was the one who received it. He said "I thought as much". She said she had never heard the Halls quarrel before, and confirmed that the poker had been bent that night.

This was corroborated by two officers who had asked her that question in their own investigation; she said she did not remember ever telling them that. She said she did not remember if Hall had his trousers and shirt on, and admitted she had had some drink that night. She did not tell her husband to clear out; he left the house when it happened and was brought back to the house by police at 11:00 on September 14th. To this, Hall said:
"When I came home on Saturday night her husband and her were there, and I went to bed."
"I never remember seeing Mr. Hall."
"Her husband was asleep. I never spoke to them. As for the poker, my son bent that by mending shoes with it. I was there in my shirt when she said I pushed her, but I did not push her."

Annie Lynch was not sworn because she had never heard of the Bible. She said that she heard Mrs. Hall saying "Do not take it out on me for the sake of the lad." She heard them curse at each other but could not hear what Mr. Hall said. When she followed her mother downstairs she saw Mr. Hall at the top of the stairs with only his shirt on; he then went to his room and put his trousers on. She told the Coroner the poker was not bent on the morning of September 12th; Hall said "She is telling an untruth". She hesitated, then said "I made a mistake, it was bent."

WJ Heslop, divisional police surgeon, said that his post-mortem had found a laceration across the top of her forehead, an inch long and extended to the bone. There was a bruise on the left side of her head two inches above he ear, and another on the right side. Her left arm and hand were badly bruised, and there was internal haemorrhaging under her right ear. Her brain was badly contused and haemorrhaged, and the cause of death was given as haemorrhage at the base of the brain. She suffered a fatty, failing heart, liver failure and a stomach ruined by alcoholism. The brain contusions were caused by blows, such as those caused by the poker or kicking. Hall said "they were new wounds", to which a juror replied "it must have been a blow that caused the fatal wound."

McCormick claimed Hall was fully dressed when she saw him leaning against the mantelpiece. Matthew Lynch said he had gotten home at 10:30pm and did not see Hall. He claimed Annie woke him shortly after 12:00, and told his wife to go downstairs. He stayed in bed until 2:00am. When he got downstairs and saw Hall's body he went to his friends' house, where he spent the day until the police called for him. A constable showed him little dents in the wall that could be caused by strikes with the poker. Hall said this was caused by killing "black jacks" (small flies).

Tram driver John Thomas Hayes (11 Staveley Street) said he was passing the house at 11:25pm, and heard a child crying "murder". He went into the house and saw Hall on a chair in the corner, bleeding, with two badly drunk women around her. This entire account was vehemently denied by Mrs. Lynch. He claimed Hall died at 11:50pm, after a Mrs. Hulme lifted her from the chair to the floor. He saw Mr. Hall, dressed, who said "I never did it". William James Hall, one of the sons, said his father had asked his mother to make him some steak, at about 6:05pm; she told him to "go to hell", and left the house. Hall then went to cook the steak himself.

Hall gave a statement:
"I was in bed and heard the baby crying, and came down for it, and there was nobody in the house only the child and my missus- I mean in the living room. The baby was on the floor crying, and I picked it up. When she saw me picking it up she was running past me to go out, and just as she was passing, I had the child in my left arm, and I gave her a clout with the back of my right hand. I never either spoke to her or nothing then; I went

upstairs. I heard Mrs. Lynch scream out, so I dressed me then and came down. Mrs. Lynch said 'whatever has tha done, Bill', and I said 'I've done nothing only give her a tap'. After that I stood there nursing the child. The holes in the wall are caused by killing beetles. The poker was bent by my son mending shoes on it."

William James was recalled and said this was true. The jury returned a verdict of wilful murder, and he was committed to the Assizes on the Coroner's warrant.

He appeared before stipendiary magistrate Francis John Headlam the same day, and was remanded until September 15th, when he was committed to the Assizes. He was charged on November 6th, before Sir Joseph Francis Leese. Mr. Foster appeared to prosecute, while Charles Pilling McKeand and Hibbert Ware defended. Evidence was given supporting Hall's sobriety and good behaviour, and Mrs. Hall's drunken and abusive personality; she had once thrown some china at him and cut his head. Elizabeth, wife of Frederick Holmes (Staveley Street), said she went into the house that night and saw Mrs. Hall sat on a chair, bleeding. She told Hall, "they say she is dead", to which he replied "no fear, she is not".

She saw the oven door open and believed Mrs. Hall had fallen on it. She knew Hall to be hard-working and Mrs. Hall to be a "dreadful woman", and believed Hall genuinely did not think he had done anything wrong. Sentence was deferred until the next morning. Baird, and Mr. Callison of the Corporation Cleansing Department, attested to his good behaviour. McKeand claimed he had been 'dragged down' over many years by the drunkenness of his wife, a bad influence on him. He asked the jury to assume, given the lack of a complete story, that Mrs. Hall was to blame, giving him the benefit of the doubt.

The jury talked for 20 minutes before coming to a judgment of manslaughter, with a strong recommendation to a merciful sentence. Sentence was deferred until the next morning. On November 10th he was sentenced, by Mr. Justice Bruce, to 3 years' penal servitude for beating his wife to death with a poker, as she had "made his life almost unendurable", and by November 18th a petition to reduce the sentence had been prepared. Places for signing the petition included the Conservative Club, Manchester Carriage Company's Office and the Alliance Inn in Harpurhey, the Blackley Post Office and the Vine Inn at Queen's Park. A special petition for signature by the jury was also prepared by Dr. Knight Coutts of Valentine House, Blackley.

56.
THE THROAT CUTTER
26 Feb 1897

John Trevelyan Hutchinson (47), a traveller for a publishing company in the Strand, London, slit his wife and 6-month-old son's throats ear-to-ear on a Friday night at their home on Berrie Road, Levenshulme, while they slept. His brother-in-law was asleep in the other room. He gave himself up to the police very early the next morning; he had written letters to the Coroner and police telling them he would kill himself, and taking the blame for the murders.

The letters were found in his pockets. He was medically examined that night, and was decided to be "weak of intellect". He was remanded at the City Police Court the next day, and re-appeared on March 1st. Superintendent Bent gave the facts of the case; when charged, he said "that is quite right". He was remanded for a week, having asked no questions in court. He appeared on March 8th, and it was found that anxiety as to his future had driven him to insanity. He was found to be insane by several doctors at the Liverpool Assizes on March 18th, and detained at Her Majesty's pleasure.

57.
THE LIVERPUDLIAN
30 Mar 1898

John McGuire (36), of 54 Christian Street, Liverpool, found employment in March 1898 by wire worker William Jones (4 Croft Street, London Road). He lodged there with him. McGuire, Jones and a bell-hanger named John Ellis were at Jones' house on the night of March 26th. They each had three pints. After talking for a while, McGuire rolled up his sleeve, slapped his muscle and said it was as hard as steel. He challenged Ellis to a fight, and Jones threw them both out. After two or three rounds of fisticuffs, Jones shouted for them to stop.

Jones heard McGuire hit the floor, but could not see what had happened because it was dark. A crowd had gathered, shouting and egging the men on. Jones and Ellis picked McGuire up and took him to lie on the sofa. He recovered a few minutes later, and Jones asked if he was hurt. He hit Jones on the back of the head and said "no". He started singing "James McGuire", and asked for a drink. Jones got him some herb beer as it was past closing time, and he drank some of it.

Jones went to bed, leaving McGuire in the kitchen. He came downstairs at 8:30am the next morning and saw McGuire trying to leave; he then sat back in the chair. 3 hours later Jones saw him shivering, and persuaded him to go to bed. He gave him some warm beer at about 12:35pm, believing him to have the "DTs" (delirium tremens, alcohol withdrawal). McGuire acted strangely, occasionally twisting and turning his head and hand.

At 6:00pm Jones sent for a doctor, who recommended he be taken to the hospital. Jones drove him to the Royal Infirmary in a cab. Ellis had disappeared. He succumbed to his wounds on March 30th. On April 5th, the City Coroner, Sydney Smelt, opened the inquest; a verdict of manslaughter was returned. Still, Ellis was missing.

Ellis was charged with manslaughter on November 10th before Mr. Justice Kennedy at the Manchester Assizes. He was undefended, prosecuted by HH Soberon and Ambrose Jones. Dr. WP Montgomery, who tended to McGuire when he was in hospital, said the injury was almost certainly due to a fall. Ellis had been found and arrested by Worcester police; when charged, he said *"I am very sorry; it was all through a drop of drink, and it was a fight in the street"*. He was found not guilty.

58.
THE CHRISTMAS QUARREL
23 Dec 1898

Groom John George Turner (29, of Great Ancoats) was drinking in a pub on Oxford Street with a girl called Nellie Ross late on a Friday night. He was talking to another man in this pub, and showed him his poniard, a long dagger, and said "this is what we use in my country, America". Turner and Ross, and another couple, left at around 11:00pm and bumped into tramway inspector Samuel Brown (Chorlton-on-Medlock) near St Peter's church. The men knew each other, and may have been friends. Brown said "Do you want a bother?".

Turner said "No, I am not in the humour", but later said "I can fight as an Englishman, if that is what you want. Beware of me, I am a Spaniard". Brown took off his coat and knocked Turner to the floor. Turner got up and stabbed Brown in the left breast with the poniard. Among the many witnesses were two employees of the Town Hall's Hackney Carriage department, Insp. Watson and Sgt. Etherington; they transported Brown to the Infirmary, which was full, so he was taken to the Salford Royal Hospital.

Turner was taken into custody. Initially the wound did not appear fatal, but Brown succumbed and died at 8:00pm on December 25th. Turner appeared at the City Police Court on December 24th. The hearing was adjourned. He appeared again on December 26th, and was remanded pending the Coroner's warrant. The Coroner's jury, in Salford, returned a verdict of guilty against Turner on December 28th. He appeared at the Manchester Assizes at 10:30am on February 1st, 1899, prosecuted by Mr. Foard and defended by Charles Pilling McKeand.

He was found guilty and sentenced to death. A letter was sent on February 6th by solicitors Hockin, Raby & Beckton to the Home Office, and by February 13th a reply had been received to the effect that the Secretary of State would reprieve him to a sentence of penal servitude for life. RD Cruikshank, of the *Manchester Courier*, went to tell Turner at Strangeways; he was greatly relieved. He told Turner that his wife had been sent to prison for assaulting Ross, and brought her to see him. They had a very happy conversation, and Turner was released from the cell.

59.
THE NEW YEAR'S BRAWL
30 Dec 1898

A Mr. Cunliffe fought with carter John Yarwood (29, of Ball Street, Liverpool Road) on a Sunday morning, December 18th, during which Yarwood hit the floor and cracked his head on the pavement. He was admitted to the Royal Infirmary and died on December 30th from brain injury.

Cunliffe was taken to the inquest, held by LJ Aitken (deputy City Coroner), on January 2nd. Mr. Jordan appeared for his defence. Dr. Montgomery gave evidence of Yarwood's time in the hospital. Other evidence suggested Cunliffe had punched Yarwood in self-defence, causing him to fall. A verdict of accidental death was returned.

He appeared before Francis John Headlam at the County Police Court later that day, and discharged.

60.
THE DEATH OF THOR
5 Mar 1899

At about 10:15pm on a Saturday night, widow Mary Thor (46) went upstairs to the room of her lodgers, joiner Francis Connolly (40) and his wife Annie, and told them to stop quarrelling. Connolly told her they were only having a little argument; they were both drunk, and were debating religion, as Connolly was a Catholic and his wife an Anglican. He offered her a beer; Thor refused. She went back to her room and shut the door at 10:30pm. At 11:00pm Thor stood at the door of her home of 8 Royle Street, Chorlton-on-Medlock and listened to a neighbour complain about the Connolly's rowing, as someone was ill next door and wanted quiet. It sounded as though the fighting had worsened.

Thor went up to tell them to be quiet for the second time that night. She told them she would give them their weeks' eviction notice if they did not stop fighting. Mr. Connolly came downstairs, leaving his wife and Thor alone in the room. He then went back upstairs to see his wife grabbing Thor by her hair on the landing. He hit Thor, then grabbed her by the waist and threw her down the stairs. She did not touch any of the stairs, instead landing straight on her head in the hallway, fracturing her skull. Two neighbours picked her up and sent for a doctor, leaving her on the kitchen floor with a pillow under her head, bleeding from one ear.

She died a few hours later from cerebral haemorrhage. This was all witnessed by Thor's daughter Ethel (9). An inquest was held at the City Coroner's Court on March 7th by Sidney Smelt. A lodger, Francis Connolly, a joiner who lived with the Thors and his wife, was present on the charge of pushing her to her death. Ethel said she saw her mother fall "flop in the lobby". Henry Jones (6

Royle Street) and Louisa Hopkins (2 Royle Street) gave evidence of the quarrel, and Thor's attempts to stop it.

Connolly claimed he and his wife were on good terms and only quarrelled in a friendly way. He claimed he had come inside the house and seen the body, and asked Ethel what had happened; she told him her mother had fallen downstairs. He said Ethel's testimony was worthless, as she was an epileptic and was not "compos mentis". He said there was no handrail on the stairs and she could have easily lost her footing. Annie Connolly claimed Thor had gone into the room and grabbed her hair. Her husband entered and dragged Thor out of the room, and then she heard a loud thud. Her husband told her Thor had fallen downstairs.

The jury returned a verdict of accidental death due to lack of evidence, and Smelt advised the police continue their investigation. Connolly was brought before Aldermen Snape and Stanley at the City Police Court the same day, and was remanded until March 7th. They were both put before Francis John Headlam at the Court, and Connolly was committed to the Assizes. Bail was allowed in two sureties of £30 each. He was brought before Mr. Justice Ridley on April 20th, undefended and prosecuted by Mr. Woodburne. Due to lack of evidence, he was discharged.

61.
THE OLD TRAFFORD SHOOTING
4 Apr 1899

At about midnight on a Monday night, electrical engineer John Percy Thompson (25) and his wife Catherine went downstairs in their home on Darnley Street, Old Trafford. She told their lodger, Catherine Fay, that he had said "a child would know its own father, but would pass its mother by". They went back up to bed, and 2 hours later he Catherine by shooting her in the back of the head, with a revolver. He calmly walked downstairs and told Fay to fetch a doctor. The police arrived and took him into custody; he remained unconcerned by the whole affair. Fay returned with a doctor at 2:45am; Catherine was on the floor with pillows under her head, and covered in bedclothes, with Thompson continuously kissing her.

The revolver was found on the floor with 5 cartridges in it, and 44 cartridges were found in his possession. He made no reply when charged with her murder. He appeared before the stipendiary magistrates at the City Police Court later that day, and was remanded. It was found that they had lived apart until a week before the murder, and he was racked with jealousy.

The Coroner's inquest was held at the City Coroner's court the next day, and returned a verdict of wilful murder. He was brought before Mr. Justice Ridley at the Manchester Assizes on April 21st, defended by Charles Pilling McKeand and prosecuted by Mr. Foard. It was proved he had recently bought the gun, and a Dr. Nesfield gave the opinion that the wound was not self-inflicted.

Fay, a nurse, said she had lodged with Catherine when she lived apart from Thompson, and had once seen him hit her. Ridley agreed with McKeand that the evidence of an abusive relationship between the Thompsons was not strong enough to convict him.

Foard reminded Ridley of Othello and Desdemona, when Desdemona's murder elicited true distress from Othello.

Ridley said *"Yes, but Desdemona was not a fact, was she? It is a proof of human nature, but nowhere reported!"*, which garnered laughter from the jury. After little deliberation the jury decided further hearing was unnecessary, and Thompson was discharged due to insufficient evidence. He was sent to an insane asylum on February 2nd, 1900.

62.
A FIGHT OUT OF HAND
4 Apr 1899

James Monks, alias Taylor (40) had lodged in an attic room in a house on Nelson Street, Rochdale Road for about a year, gaining a miserable income as a wood-chopper while his wife worked as a charwoman. They were described as quiet and inoffensive, and shared their room with another family, separated by a partition, as well as their house. The man was a stonemason named Thomas Read, and the woman was named Madden. They had moved in 5 days prior to the murder. On Monday, April 3rd, Read quarrelled with another female lodger (probably Madden, or his girlfriend). He was asked by the Monks to quiet down, which he refused to do and used threatening language towards them.

Early in the morning on April 4th, Mrs. Monks went out to work, leaving James in bed. At about 2:00pm Madden saw him sitting in the kitchen. A few minutes later he went upstairs and quarrelled with Read in the attic. He was hit on the head with a padlock, and fell to the floor, when Read began kicking him. Madden heard someone hit the floor, and the Monks' infant son begin screaming. The couple ran out of the house, and another lodger, Mr. Peacock, ran upstairs to see Monks unconscious and battered, lying on his bed. There were several wounds on his head and blood on the walls and floor. It appeared from the blood that he had been severely beaten in a corner of the room, and then lifted onto the bed.

Between 2:00pm and 3:00pm, a police constable on duty on Rochdale Road was informed by some children of a fight between two men in a house on nearby Nelson Street. He went to the house and found Monks on the bed. He arranged for him to be taken to the Infirmary, and he was pronounced dead upon arrival due to brain haemorrhage. Further police inquiries discovered Monks' identity. Peacock and Madden informed the Chief Police office, and constables and officers were sent to search for the fugitives; the man was described as a darker-skinned foreigner.

Monks' son told police that he had seen his father being beaten about the head with a padlock. At 11:00pm, Thomas Read was arrested by Inspector Hargreaves. An inquest was held at the City Coroner's Court the next day, with Mrs. Monks being charged as an accessory after the fact and Read with the murder.
He was committed for trial on April 14th; his girlfriend was also charged, but was dismissed. He appeared before Mr. Justice Ridley at the Manchester Assizes on April 28th, and was sentenced to death for the murder, but by May 5th the sentence had been commuted to penal servitude for life.

63.
THE PENKNIFE IN BESWICK
22 Aug 1899

Engraver Thomas Henry Ridley (29) lived at 11 Sandown Street, Beswick, with his wife Jennie, of seven years, and their two children. On a Tuesday morning he told her she would be dead by 5:30pm that day. Throughout the morning and afternoon he muttered to himself and acted very strangely. That afternoon, she was washing in the yard when her husband ran at her as if to strike her. She ran into the house, and he went up behind her and put an arm around her, feigning an apology; instead, he attempted to murder her by slitting her throat with a penknife. She screamed and ran to the next house.

They helped her back into her house and put her on the couch. He was immediately apologetic and asked someone to fetch a doctor. Inspector Davenport arrived and arrested him, taking him to Brook Street station. His shirt front and coat were covered in blood, as was the pillow and bed. There was some blood in the yard. Mrs. Ridley was taken to Ancoats Hospital in a dangerous condition. He was brought before the magistrates at the City Police Court the next day.

Davenport, representing the police, gave formal evidence and told the court of the doctors' opinion that the injury was very serious. He was remanded until August 30th, with the hopes that Mrs. Ridley would be well enough to attend court by then. On August 30th, Mrs. Ridley also appeared to prosecute her husband, swathed in bandages. He was defended by Mr. Burton, and was "respectably dressed". Davenport, replying to Burton, denied that Ridley had apologised for the assault, or claimed his wife provoked him. He had said nothing about his wife's drinking or absence.

Mrs. Ridley gave her evidence quietly to the clerk, Mr. Robson. She said her husband had showed her the knife a week before and told her it was "sharp enough to cut anybody's off". Burton added that she had told him she was not in the habit of drinking and absenting from the house, and did not call him names or quarrel with him.

He appeared before Mr. Justice Kennedy at the Manchester Assizes on November 13th, with Mr. Foard prosecuting and Charles Pilling McKeand defending him. The jury returned a verdict of wounding with intent to do grievous bodily harm; McKeand mentioned that Ridley had been in prison for three months prior to this. The judge remarked on the horrible nature of the crime and Ridley's luck that he had not killed her. He was sentenced to 5 years of penal servitude.

64.
THE POOR GIRL OF CRUMPSALL
22 Aug 1899

Theresa Jackson (14) lived with her drunken parents and younger sister in a filthy house at 2 Spinner's Row, Crumpsall. Her mother, Mary Ellen, worked with her in a wireworks in Blackley. The girl had been ill for some months and bedbound since the last week of July. Her parents neglected her, allowing her to sleep on bags and taking her food and drink. She died in bed early on a Tuesday morning and was found at 8:30pm by her parents, covered in vermin and maggots. The majority of the facts surrounding the death, which seems to be a result of her squalid living conditions, were made apparent at the inquest, held by LJ Aitken at the City Coroner's Court on August 30th, watched by a Mr. Hokin for the NSPCC.

Her mother identified the body. A neighbour, Martha Yates, said she had given Jackson some clean clothes to sleep on rather than bags, and had taken her food, but it was eaten by her parents. The night before she died her parents were drunk and fighting. Yates brought her some brandy and soda and a bowl of soup, but her parents took that as well. The bedclothes were so filthy they had to be burned. She told Hockin she had not been cared for at all during her time ill in bed.

Sarah Ridley (14 Spinner's Row) said she had donated milk and bedclothes to Theresa, and claimed that the parents' fighting on the previous night was so bad that the door had to be tied shut with a clothes line by the neighbours to stop them disturbing her. Mary Ann Dale (1 Spinner's Row) said she had known the family since December 1898, and claimed the parents "were always drunk". She was with her when she died. Aitken asked Mr. Jackson if the other daughter was injured; he said she was

in a children's club, but did not know if it was good or not. The parents were in such a filthy state that the floor of the courtroom had to be sprinkled with disinfectant due to the smell.
NSPCC Inspector Thomas Speers said he had visited the house and was overwhelmed by the stench. Police surgeon Dr. Heslop said the body was swarming with maggots, with tuberculosis in both lungs; the only thing keeping her alive was the meagre amount of food she had been given. Her stomach and intestines were practically empty. Neither parent gave a statement, and both were found guilty of manslaughter.

On November 16th, the Jacksons were brought before Mr. Justice Kennedy at the Manchester Assizes, defended by Mr. Gibbon and prosecuted by Mr. Overend Evans. It was revealed that shortly before she died, her parents had taken the few coppers she had saved from under her pillow and spent it on drink. Gibbon said the entire income of the family was £1 per week from Mr. Jackson.

His defence revolved around the theory that inaction is not action, and there was little evidence of ill-treatment. He said the jury should consider that the neglect was not criminal. Kennedy, in summing up, referred to the lifestyle and ignorance of the Jacksons, and asked the jury to take into account that the Jacksons were not under normal circumstances; they were very poor, with squalid states of life. The jury found Mrs. Jackson guilty, and discharged Mr. Jackson. Sentence was deferred until November 18th, when she was given 10 months' hard labour.

65.
THE BROTHER AND THE BROOMSTICK
16 Oct 1899

John Henry Riley (24, of 15 Molyneux Street, Chorlton-on-Medlock) was a farrier, employing his 14-year-old brother Albert (21 Upper West Grove, Chorlton) as his apprentice. Between 4:00pm and 4:30pm on a Monday afternoon, Albert played on Molyneux Street with Arthur Jackson (17, of Earl Street, Longsight). Jackson was washing a van in the yard at Riley's house, and Albert made fun of him for "walking a bit funny". Jackson said something rude, causing John to come out and chastise him. John then went back into the house.

Albert laughed at Jackson, and John was about to return to tell Albert off. Seeing his brother, he ran towards the gate, and John threw a piece of a broken broomstick at him. This caused a wound a little over ¼" long, an eighth across and 1½" deep on the back of his neck, leading to a fatal haemorrhage at the base of the brain. John and Robert Lawrie lifted him up and took him into the house. They found some brandy and fetched a doctor, but he died a few minutes later.

An inquest was held at the City Coroner's Court by Sidney Smelt on October 18th. Jackson said he had heard Albert fall over from the other side of the van, and insisted he had never had a knife. A Mrs. Embleton said she saw Albert fall against a stone placed at the gateway, then roll over. Dr. Heslop gave a medical analysis of the death, and believed it was caused by a penknife or fine chisel. John claimed that he was in the kitchen when he heard Albert cry, "Oh!", and that he found Albert lying face-down near the wooden gates at the yard entrance. No witnesses called could explain the wound. Smelt remarked it was an awkward case, but that it was certainly a stabbing and could not be dropped. He adjourned the case until October 24th.

On November 14th, the case was put before Mr. Justice Kennedy at the Manchester Assizes. John confessed to throwing the broomstick and causing the wound. Charles Pilling McKeand, defending him, argued that manslaughter and murder are very different things and vary in degrees. He said the wound was a 1-in-1000 chance, and called the death a "misadventure". John was discharged.

66.
THE UNHAPPY LODGERS
10 Nov 1899

At about 3:30pm on a Tuesday afternoon, November 4th, fellow lodgers Mrs. Eliza Sharples, John Henry Watson (33) and hawker William Cooper (28) were in the front kitchen of their home of 289 Great Ancoats Street. Both men were drunk. Cooper said "Jack, give me a penny for some beer". Watson refused, and Cooper said "give me a smoke". He kept pestering Watson until Watson threatened to hit him. He was cutting tobacco with a knife, and said "if you do not go away I will run the knife into you". He then stabbed Cooper twice in the chest. PC Mountford arrested him; he said "I would not have done it, but he plagued me so". He later found the knife in the fireplace.

Cooper was admitted to Ancoats Hospital. Watson appeared at the County Police Court on November 6th on a charge of causing grievous bodily harm. Cooper gave a statement on November 9th, and died on the morning of November 10th. The inquest was held on the morning of November 13th by deputy Coroner LJ Aitken at the City Coroner's Court. John Cooper, his father, identified the body. Thomas Sherrat, another lodger, said there had been "bad blood" between them for some time; Cooper had once spent 14 days in prison for kicking Watson, and was known as a mean drunk.

Dr. Crompton, senior house surgeon at the hospital, said Cooper was unconscious upon admission, haemorrhaging from the wound. There was an incised wound an inch long on his right breast and a puncture wound on the left, which had set up acute septic pericarditis. This was given as the cause of death. Deputy judicial clerk Joseph Hyde read Cooper's statement, which had been taken in a magistrate's presence; it left out the fact that he had repeatedly bothered Watson. The jury returned a verdict of manslaughter.

He was brought before stipendiary magistrate Francis John Headlam at the County Police Court, with evidence from the inquest being repeated. Watson was committed for trial at the Liverpool Assizes. He appeared on December 6th, prosecuted by Charles Pilling McKeand and defended by Mr. Oulton and was found not guilty, having acted in self-defence and out of fear, with great provocation.

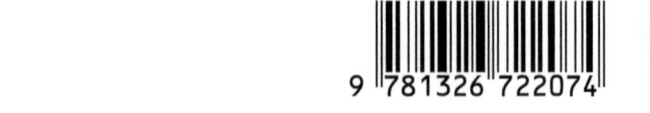

Lightning Source UK Ltd.
Milton Keynes UK
UKHW021848060422
401197UK00005B/135